LAUDERDALE COUNTY
MISSISSIPPI

LAUDERDALE COUNTY MISSISSIPPI

A BRIEF HISTORY

RICHELLE PUTNAM

THE History PRESS

Published by The History Press
Charleston, SC 29403
www.historypress.net

Cover images: Downtown with a view of the Dough Boy and Strand Theater. *Courtesy of Lauderdale County Department of Archives and History*; Dentzel Carousel. *Author's collection.*

First published 2011

Manufactured in the United States

ISBN 978.1.60949.021.8

Library of Congress Cataloging-in-Publication Data

Putnam, Richelle.
Lauderdale County, Mississippi : a brief history / Richelle Putnam.
p. cm.
Includes bibliographical references.
ISBN 978-1-60949-021-8
1. Lauderdale County (Miss.)--History. 2. Lauderdale County (Miss.)--Social conditions. I. Title.
F347.L3P88 2011
976.2'676--dc23
2011042015

CONTENTS

FOREWORD

You hold in your hands a fabulous gem. Lauderdale County has a vivid, dramatic history that has, for a very long time, deserved to be told. That day has come.

Richelle Putnam, our storyteller in residence, has combed articles, news clippings, photographs and any other scrap of information she could get her hands on. Lauderdale County is fortunate that a writer of Richelle's talents and diligence chose to write this history. The level of research, analysis and editing that went into this project is tremendous. This is her climax.

You are about to embark on a journey to a place with deep entrepreneurial roots and a strong community bond. Lauderdale County has, for decades, been held together by its strength of community, profound generosity and everlasting entrepreneurial spirit.

This was witnessed firsthand when Hurricane Katrina devastated Lauderdale County and every basic human need had to be provided on an unprecedented scale. We simply were not prepared for that kind of disaster 150 miles inland.

But Lauderdale County stepped to the plate. It took care of its own and many evacuees who made their way here. It took them in. It gave them shelter, warmth, food, medical care and other necessities. Many of the evacuees made Lauderdale County their home.

The reason the community of Lauderdale County was able to handle that level of disaster relief is because we are no strangers to helping one another.

We do it every day. Whether it is through one of our several nonprofits, our churches reaching out or our business leaders banding together for a common cause, community bond is our standard.

Since serving as mayor of Meridian, this has become even more apparent to me. I have had the chance to work with other bodies of government and organizations on a whole new level.

I have also had the honor of getting to know Richelle over the past two years. We are truly blessed that she calls Lauderdale County home.

Mayor Cheri Barry

ACKNOWLEDGEMENTS

This book is the work of many, from the record keepers of centuries past to the historians who breathed life into those records for readers to enjoy and learn from. To the following, I am deeply grateful:

The Mississippi Department of Archives and History, the Lauderdale County Department of Archives and History, Meridian Public Library, the City of Meridian, Wesley House, Citizens National Bank, the Phil Hardin Foundation, Ross Collins Vocational Building and Meridian Public Schools Administration, whose on-site records played a crucial part in securing the accuracy of this book. Ward Calhoun and Leslie Joyner, for sacrificing their precious time to steer me to information and photographs. Meridian mayor Cheri Barry, who supported and encouraged me in this project, and the many Lauderdale County residents who contributed oral histories and photographs. My dear friend June Davidson, who traveled many roads and dug through dusty papers with me. David and Donnie Roddie, Ralph and Pat Gordon and Sheila Hutcherson, whose friendships have been great supportive beams in my life. My sister, Robyn, who has always been my encourager. My husband, Tim, the miracle and love of my life, who never doubts me. My children, Eric, Erin, Bailey and John, who loved me even when my eyes and fingers were permanently attached to my computer. My grandchildren, Lance, Brett, Brittany, Brianne and Ava Marie, for simply being who they are. Tim Putnam Jr. and Jennifer Putnam-Ripley, who held me up during my weakest moments. And last, but also most, my mother, Doris Gamble, who taught me to value each person in this world and how to find the good in every situation and to see what's right before determining what's wrong—in anything.

IN THE BEGINNING

The Choctaws

Before the establishment of the Mississippi Territory, villages of the Choctaws existed throughout what would become Lauderdale County, with major settlements in Alamucha (Old Town), Chunky-Chitto (Chunkey-Chitto), Toomsuba (Taissuba), Okatibbee (Okaittibih), Kewanee and the Koosa (Koonsha, Coosha) Towns.

In *Indian Towns and Trails in Lauderdale County and Adjacent Counties* by W.G. Allison, the trail on Danville's map of 1732 leads from the old trading route at the Chickasawhay in Clarke County to "Concha-Tchitou, the Great Village of Canes," in the southwest corner of Lauderdale County, somewhere along the Chunky Creek.

The History of Daleville, Mississippi states that "Kushak" or "Kusha" was a Choctaw term that applied to reed-brake, as well as reed, and is spelled "Coucha" on Decreney's map of 1733. On Roman's map of 1775, it is spelled "Coosha." Fred Edminston, in *Lauderdale: The Empire County, Early Years 1830–1865*, uses Kunshak and Coonsha. Concha has also been a spelling. The most used English spelling for the largest town in the Choctaw Nation was probably "Koonsha," but for this book, the spelling "Coosha" will be used.

In northern Lauderdale County, near present-day Naval Air Station (NAS) and a few miles from Daleville, where Choctaws often camped around springs and waterways located there, Coosha was a notable town of approximately twelve hundred, extending for two and a half miles along a bluff over little Lost Horse Creek, where fish, deer, turkeys, squirrels and

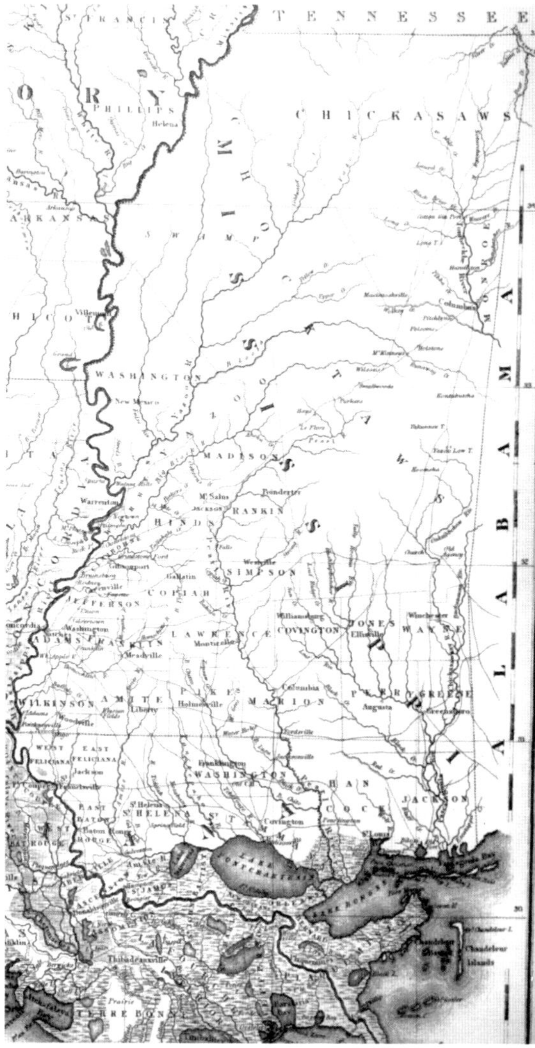

1828 map. *Courtesy of Mississippi Department of Archives and History.*

other game were abundant in the dense canebrake between the forks of the stream. Supposedly, this was a favorite hiding place for horse thieves, so the Choctaws named the creek Lost Horse Creek. Thickets of plums and garden plots—which included maize, or corn, a favorite crop of the Native Americans—separated the cluster of hamlets that formed the town governed by Chief Pushmataha. Approximately a mile and a half from Lockhart, close to the eastern edge of town, a large knoll served as a burial ground, and here some of Pushmataha's family members were buried. A leading figure among the Coosha people was Oklahoma, who for a brief period served as Mingo of the Six Town District. At the death of Oklahoma in 1846, Coosha Town was abandoned and overtaken by bushes and vines.

A few miles east of Coosha on Ponta Creek, at the present site of Lauderdale, was the village of Pante (Panthe). From here, Choctaw settlements spread into Kemper County and formed the villages of Okalusa (Black Water), Shomo Takali or Shumotakali (Hanging Horse), Hankha Ula or Haanka Ullah (Wild Goose There Cries), Holihta asha or Olitassa (Fort Is There), Iyanabi or Avanabi (Ironwood) and Coonchitto, one of the largest towns, being called by the French "the village of the Great Chief."

Into Neshoba County, there was Cushtusha (the Place of Fleas), Boucfouca (Surrounded by Bayous) and Yashu. Newton County included Oka Hulla (Beloved Water), Chanki Chitto (Big Chanki) and Oskilakna (Yellow Canes).

Major Choctaw towns were connected by trails branching into all directions to the territories of the surrounding tribes. The Great Trading Path, running north from Mobile and crossing Lost Horse Creek about two hundred yards below the convergence of the two prongs, penetrated Coosha Town on the east. One prong flowed northeast, and the other went into "Holihtasha," or Fort Town. The Six Town Trail extended from the Chickasaw Country into Jasper County and was the main road from the south leading to the famous Dancing Rabbit Spring. Paths to the Tombigbee River used by American soldiers during the Creek War were of great military importance. One ran from Holihtasha at Dekalb westward through what is now the city of Jackson and on the Mississippi, near Vicksburg. This trail was used by General Jackson in marching his troops to New Orleans.

Early history of east central Mississippi and much of the Tombigbee River basin includes historical accounts of Frenchmen Pierre and Charles Juzan, half brothers from Mobile, Alabama, who, toward the end of the Revolutionary War, settled in the Choctaw Nation in the Mississippi Territory and married Choctaw women. Pierre settled in an Indian village north of Hickory known as Chunky (Chunkey) Chitto, while Charles Juzan married Pushmataha's niece and put down roots at Coosha Town, near Lost Horse Creek, about four miles southeast of present-day Lizelia. Charles

Juzan's home was located on Gaines Trace at the crossroads where the "old road" ran southwest to northeast. The brothers established thriving trading posts at Chunky Chitto, Coosha Town and Tuscahoma, where the hides and fur from the territory's abundant game of mink, otter and deer were exchanged for guns, gunpowder, ammunition, knives, blankets, metal wares and glass beads used for garment and body ornamentation. These prized pelts were then transported to Mobile or New Orleans ports to be shipped to France and converted into fancy coats and finery for French nobility. The Juzans entertained travelers and bartered alcoholic beverages, which quickly exerted an addictive power over the Choctaw people, as it had over many white settlers. On July 2, 1838, Oklahoma and his wife, Anun Tooner, sold to Phebe (Phoebe) Juzan five acres of land located near present-day Lockhart, close to where Wild Horse Creek enters Lost Horse Creek.

But Indian nations in the new territory weren't to be tolerated. In his message of 1829, Mississippi governor Gerard C. Brandon declared that the prosperity of the state was retarded by such vast portions of fertile lands remaining in the possession of "savage tribes of Indians, who, as they progress in civilization, become attached to the soil and cannot be induced to remove by the policy heretofore used of treating them as a sovereign people, and will, eventually set up for themselves a government, professing to be an independent sovereignty within our limits, in defiance of the authority of the state."

And on December 6, 1830, President Andrew Jackson's annual message to Congress was:

> *The consequences of a speedy removal will be important to the United States, to individual States, and to the Indians themselves…It will place a dense and civilized population in large tracts of country now occupied by a few savage hunters…It will separate the Indians from immediate contact with settlements of whites; free them from the power of the States; enable them to pursue happiness in their own way and under their own rude institutions; will retard the progress of decay, which is lessening their numbers, and perhaps cause them gradually, under the protection of the Government and through the influence of good counsels, to cast off their savage habits and become an interesting, civilized, and Christian community…What good man would prefer a country covered with forests and ranged by a*

> *few thousand savages to our extensive Republic, studded with cities, towns, and prosperous farms, embellished with all the improvements which art can devise or industry execute, occupied by more than 12,000,000 happy people, and filled with all the blessings of liberty, civilization, and religion?*

The irony of the government's attitude toward so-called Indian savagery was its blind disregard to the white saloonkeepers and gamblers, portable wagon bars, frontier roughnecks and prostitutes who caused excessive mayhem in the settlements. Further irony had Secretary of War John Eaton ordering all missionaries away from the treaty grounds because they were cautioning the Choctaws not to be cheated by anyone, even the American government.

Where present-day Noxubee County lies was a ridge between the two prongs of Dancing Rabbit Creek, about one hundred yards west of the well-known spring that bears the same name as the creek. The larger, eastern creek was known as the Big Rabbit, and the western rivulet was Little Rabbit. A nearby natural spring was a popular watering hole. This area had been a well-used hunting ground of the Choctaws. Six Town Trail ran by this spring and through what would soon be Lauderdale County, passing near modern-day Chunky as it led to New Orleans. The Choctaw called these waters *Chukfi ahihla bok*, or "Creek Where the Rabbit Dances."

Major John H. Eaton and General John Coffee of Tennessee, close friends of President Andrew Jackson, were the commissioners, and they were instructed by the president to "fail not to make a treaty." General George Strother Gaines was to collect enough provisions for three thousand persons for one week. Mingoes Greenwood Leflore, Mushulatubbee and Nittakechi, nephew of Pushmataha, had one camp while the people had another.

Chief David Folsom and his Christian party dedicated their evenings to signing and prayer but were driven away by the commissioners. Others utilized the gambling tables and drinking places opened by the white commoners and allowed by the commissioners. On September 18, the talks began. John Pitchlyn served as Major Eaton's interpreter, whose final statement was:

> *After the present time, we shall no more offer to treat with you. You have seen commissioners from our country for the last time. Hereafter, you will be left to yourselves and to the laws of the States within which you reside;*

> *and, when weary of them, your nation must remove as it can and at its own expense.*

The Treaty of Dancing Rabbit Creek served as a model for treaties of removal for the Chickasaw, Cherokee, Creek and Seminole tribes and was the first land exchange to be negotiated under the Indian Removal Act, signed by the Choctaw Nation on September 27, 1830. The terms of said treaty ceded control of over 11 million acres in exchange for control over 15 million acres in Oklahoma, known simply as Indian Territory.

Folsom, who had been instrumental in missionary work and providing schools and smithies to the Choctaws, wrote to the Presbyterian ministers in the nation, "We are exceedingly tired. We have just heard of the ratification of the Choctaw Treaty. Our doom is sealed. There is no other course for us but to turn our faces to our new homes toward the setting sun."

The January 18, 1837 report from the Committee on Private Land Claims to the U.S. Senate admitted that there were instances of neglect in registering names of Indians who had signified their desire to stay and become citizens of the state within the prescribed time frame. Gabriel and Grant Lincecum both attested to this. The committee's findings and conclusions directed the War Department to order all aggrieved Choctaws to present their evidence and be awarded the land as entitled. Approximately 520 heads of Choctaw families filed claims.

The census taken just after the Treaty of Dancing Rabbit Creek reported that there were 19,554 persons in the Choctaw Nation. Of that number, approximately 15,000 moved west, leaving fewer than 4,500 in Mississippi.

In the words of Choctaw George W. Harkins, "We as Choctaws rather chose to suffer and be free, than live under the degrading influence of laws, which our voice could not be heard in their formation…We go forth sorrowful, knowing that wrong has been done."

THE TERRITORY

As a result of the treaty, all remaining Choctaw lands were surrendered to the United States, whereby the following Mississippi counties would be established: Noxubee, Kemper, Lauderdale, Clarke, Oktibbeha, Winston, Choctaw, Tallahatchie, Yalobusha, Carroll, Jasper, Neshoba, Smith, Scott, Leake and Attala. Through the 1832 Treaty of Pontotoc, the Chickasaws relinquished their land in northeastern Mississippi.

Established on December 23, 1833, Lauderdale County, Mississippi, included an area of approximately nineteen townships, known as "all the territory within townships 5, 6, 7 and 8, of ranges 14, 15, 16, 17, 18 and 19," consisting of approximately 715 square miles and named for Colonel James Lauderdale, a Tennessean of John Coffee's mounted brigade who was killed on December 23, 1814, in New Orleans during the night attack on the British.

The diverse topography of Mississippi ranges from just above sea level (Gulf Coast area) to its highest elevation of 805 feet (Woodall Mountain, Tishomingo County) and includes seven geographic regions in two distinct plains. The Delta Region lies in the Mississippi Alluvial Plain. The East Gulf Coastal Plain, which covers most of Mississippi, includes the Loess Bluffs and Brown Loam Hills, the Red Clay Hills, the Prairies, the Northeast Highlands, the Piney Woods and the Gulf Coast. According to *Wildflowers of Mississippi* by S. Lee Timme, these regions are further broken down into nine regions and one subregion relative to geological formations, topography and soils. They are listed as Coastal, Pine Hills, Loess Hills, Jackson Prairies, North Central Plains, Mississippi Alluvial Plain, Flatwoods, Pontotoc Hills, Black Prairie and Fall Line Hills. Per these regions, Lauderdale County is located in the North Central Plains region, with the northeast tip reaching into the Flatwoods region.

The North Central Plains region is hilly with some ridges, its soil containing silt, loam, sand and clay. Covered by a variety of woody plants such as hickory, oak, persimmon, elm, wild plum, sassafras, witch hazel, hydrangea, sumac and wild grapes, the majority of tree growth is loblolly and shortleaf pine. Indigenous plants paint the landscape throughout the year with buttercups, bluets, milkweeds, anemone, morning glories, wild petunia, asters and sunflowers. In the lowlands, beneath the oak, maple, elm, river birch, bald cypress and sycamore, grow phlox, bellworts, fringed orchids, meadow beauties, rattlebox and Japanese honeysuckle.

The Flatwoods region consists of clay and sand on flat to slightly hilly land with the same plant growth of the North Central Plains.

In southern Lauderdale County, bordered to the north by Interstate 20/59 and to the south by Interstate 10, as reported by the Mississippi Arts Commission's Folk Life, Folk Artist Project, the Piney Woods region is part of a larger geographical region in the southeast United States.

Located in East Central Mississippi, Lauderdale County is surrounded by Kemper, Neshoba, Newton and Clarke Counties and borders the Alabama line. Coupled with a semitropical climate and diverse rich loam soil, the geography supported the principal lifestyle of agriculture that lasted for over a century.

Lauderdale County's terrain consists of twenty-six sedimentary soils divided into three defined soil divisions: upland or old sedimentary soils, recent stream alluvium (first bottom and frequently overflowed soils) and, finally, old stream alluvium (second bottom soils located above normal overflow). Numerous small streams trickle off the Chickasawhay and Tombigbee Rivers and other larger waterways like the Alamucha, Chunky, Tallahatta, Okatibbee, Chickasawhay, Sowashee and Ponta Creeks. The county's red clay hills are named for the red color of the soil and large clay deposits.

Fed by Dry and Chickasawhay Creeks, Okatibbee Stream begins in Kemper County close to the Neshoba County line. The Tallahatta Stream empties into the Chunky River, which, about two miles east of Chunky, enters Lauderdale County. Ponta Creek enters Lauderdale County from Kemper County; Lost Horse Creek starts near Lockhart, Mississippi; and Baker's Creek begins at the old Cooper Spring in Daleville. Sowashee Creek flows south, emptying into Okatibbee Creek. Alamucha Creek flows into the Little Alamucha, which in turn flows into the Tombigbee River. In addition to these water sources, Lauderdale County possesses numerous Artesian wells, the majority being found off Highway 80 near Meehan at the Newton County line.

Mineral springs also run through other regions of Lauderdale County, such as the freestone water spring located on the Old Cooper Institute at Daleville. In early times, troughs inside the house were placed over this spring, and the running water kept milk and butter cool for the boarders. Located within the yellow loam region, where important sulfur and chalybeate springs were known for quality as well as quantity, Lauderdale Springs once housed a large hotel where travelers enjoyed the cool, clear water and the medicinal effects from the sulfuric atmosphere.

Near Daleville, the soil is a stiff, red clay loam, deficient in humus but productive. The community of Lauderdale possesses the roughest landforms, but some flat areas could be utilized for agriculture. South of Marion, productivity is only fair due to soil of yellow sandy loam. In Meridian and southward, whitish sandy soils hinder productivity because of the rapid, broken erosion. With an average rainfall of fifty-three inches, Lauderdale County's eight-month growing season delays the first killing frost until around the first week in November, with winter's last frost showing up around mid-March. January is the coldest month, and temperatures are hottest in July and August.

SETTLERS AND SETTLEMENTS

Settlers usually arrived in groups, bringing with them a few cattle and sheep. Their first task was to build shelter and then clear a path to the nearest settlement. Pine log houses were floored with puncheons made by split-in-half pine logs with the flat side turned up and smoothed. The square nails used were slightly tapered from the head to the end. Kitchen floors of clay were packed level with mauls. Chimneys were constructed of one- to two-inch-thick wooden strips split from pines and stacked to form the skeleton of the chimney. Clay was mixed with coarse grass and wetted to a thick consistency, then placed between the layers of sticks inside and out. To prepare the land for planting, horses, mule or oxen dragged plows across the land to pull up tree roots and rocks and to loosen the soil.

The U.S. Surveyor's Office in Jackson commissioned James Oswald, John B. Peyton, Frederick I. Bowie, William P. Stone, Henry Hamblin, George Dougharty, Jacob B. Womack and William L. Dearing to conduct land surveys in Lauderdale County to prepare for new residents. These surveys thoroughly described land and included details such as streams, vegetation, soil and terrains, existing homesteads and cultivated fields.

Early immigrants into the county included William Chandler, who, on December 13, 1834, bought 40 acres at the Land Office in Augusta, Mississippi. William Henderson bought 68 acres at the site in Old Marion on December 10, 1834, and on September 5, 1838, James Keeton bought this land and an additional 418 acres from at least three other individuals.

Historical sign, frontiersman Sam Dale. *Author's collection.*

On March 10, 1837, L.B. Bains bought from William and Martha Stokes land located about two miles northeast of where Bailey is today.

In mid-1836, the state auditor reported that 1,830 free persons and 760 "colored" people lived in Lauderdale County. One year later, there were 1,883 whites and 544 slaves. There was 3,425 cultivated acres that had produced 128 bales of cotton.

Samuel Dale was born in 1772 to Scotch-Irish parents Samuel and Mary O'Brian Dale in Rockbridge County, Virginia. Six feet, two inches tall, broad shouldered and muscular, Dale was known for his ability to maneuver quietly and lightly, much like a Native American, and is remembered for his legendary "Canoe Fight" against the Creeks in 1813.

On November 21, 1831, Sam Dale purchased for $700 from the Choctaw Ia-cha-hopa his reserve of two sections of land, approximately 1,280 acres in present-day Lizelia, close to the old Choctaw town of Pante, or in today's term, Ponta. According to *Sam Dale, Southern Pioneer*, Dale and Ia-cha-hopa were blood brothers, and their oath to each other promised that "as long as the sun shines, the moon and stars rise in the heavens, the grass grows green and the rivers run to the sea, we will be friends, and where one is buried the other will be buried."

Often, homeless Choctaws camped around Dale's plantation and lived off his land. Samuel Dale died on May 24, 1841.

Richard McLemore, born in South Carolina (some histories have recorded his birthplace as Virginia, but the 1850 U.S. census recorded it as South Carolina) on September 21, 1798, was married to Nancy Perry Hill and had nine children. In 1831, he received a Federal Land Grant of approximately two thousand acres, which later became part of Lauderdale County. His home of hewn logs consisted of a long hall with stone chimneys at both ends and was located on the road leading from Lauderdale to Enterprise, where the current Eleventh Street crosses Eighteenth Avenue. Daughter Sarah, born in 1833, was the first recorded white birth in Lauderdale County.

His nearest neighbor being eight to ten miles away, McLemore enticed potentially good neighbors into the area by offering them free land. Part of McLemore's plantation was his cotton gin. This place, then referred to as Gin-Lot field, is the present location of the Lauderdale County Courthouse.

The Progress Report of 1831–1962, "Citizens of Color" in Meridian, Mississippi, added that

> *in 1831, Richard McLemore migrated from South Carolina, with some of his slaves to clear a plantation on the present site of Meridian. These dark-skinned toilers of the soil, worked diligently for the area's earliest "pioneer," and* [McLemore] *was offering land free to white settlers he thought would make desirable neighbors. The Negroes' strong backs and tireless limbs became important now as* [McLemore] *was to clear the paths for what was to make Meridian an important transportation center—the rails.*

Virginian Jubal B. Hancock and his Choctaw wife and children relocated to Mississippi to live among his wife's people. Because Hancock was a white citizen of the United States and his wife was not head of the house, neither he nor his wife was entitled to receive any land available to Choctaws under the Treaty of Dancing Rabbit Creek. According to Frank Durr, a former slave who wrote about Lauderdale County's early history, Jubal Hancock submitted his claim for 640 acres of land on behalf of his wife and for their children, 320 acres each for William and Mary and 160 acres for Caroline. After a twelve-year-long legal battle, on August 11, 1842, the Hancocks received their land under Article 14 of the treaty.

Records reveal that Jewish life in Lauderdale County began in the town of Marion. David Rosenbaum purchased land in Marion in 1837 and joined

Ole Stennis Place, 7812 King Road, built in 1857 by Hays Rodgers and sold in 1869 to Adam T. Stennis, great-uncle to U.S. senator John C. Stennis. It is known to be the oldest home in Lauderdale County. *Author's collection.*

Isaac Rosenbaum in the business partnership of D. & I. Rosenbaum. The families of Abraham Threefoot, Isaac Rosenbaum, Leopold Rosenbaum, E. Lowenstein and Jacob Cohen also lived in Marion during the early years. Jacob Meyer moved his family from Kosciusko to Marion.

Family Maps of Lauderdale County records the early 1841 settlements, settlers and important waterways in Lauderdale County as follows:

Settlers with the surnames of Ford, Edwards, Barnes, Holiman, Cooper, Osborn, Savell, Calhoun, Russell, Coats and Crory purchased land in what would be the village of Suqualena, where Suqualena and Cedar Grove Cemeteries now lie. Suqualena Creek and Harper Creek ran through these sections. Suqualena, located nine miles northwest of Meridian, was founded in 1840. Suqualena is an Indian name for Poor Hog and was home to one of the oldest schools: Pinkney Vaughn School. The post office opened on July 23, 1851.

The Pine Springs, Hookston, Nellieburg and Bailey area in 1841 included the Coats, Calhouns and Fords, as well as the Lewis, Boon, Prier, Evans,

Hatcher, Lee, Campbell, Stokes, Howell, McWooten, Stokes, Hubbard, Eubanks, Hamrick, Thornton, Young, Mott, Kennedy, Canady and Ward families. Okatibbee Creek, Suqualena Creek, Harper Creek, Rogers Creek, Bailey Branch Creek, Gunn Branch Creek, Gallagher Creek and Loper Creek ran through these communities. In Hookston, William A. Hooks was postmaster of the post office established on December 23, 1884. Hookston was located approximately eight miles northwest of Meridian. Bailey is located approximately twelve miles north of Meridian. Its population in 1900 was fifty-six. The post office was established on July 18, 1833. Nellieburg was located five miles northwest of Meridian. When the Meridian & Bigbee Railroad was built in 1913, a station was constructed here and was named after Nellie Sharman Schley, the wife of railroad president J.T. Schley. Pine Springs was five miles northeast of Meridian.

In the Houston, Marion and Poplar Springs area, early names were Chester, Stanton, Odom, Tabb, Gillaspie, Sikes, Mott, Wilson, Chester, Finnen, Tabb, Alexander, Jordan, Wood, Thornton, Crane, Grant, Ballard, Philips, Tinnin, Hall, Keeton, Richardson, Dunn, Hails, Chandler, McLemore (Richard), McCann, McMullan, Miller, Lewis, McDow, Ulrick, Ramsay, Cains, Howell, Warbington and Berrien (1840). Through these sections ran Gunn Creek, Robbins Creek, McLemore Creek, Sowashee Creek, Nanabe Creek and Brandon Branch. Marion was the first county seat of Lauderdale County. The old Marion Post Office was established on May 27, 1837. Marion Station Post Office was established on January 25, 1867. Lucile, known also as the Poplar Springs community, was a place for picnics and social gatherings around Thirty-ninth Street and Poplar Springs Drive, where many poplar trees grew around a large hollow where a clear spring ran. Its post office, named Lucile, was established in 1891. The community became part of Meridian in 1927 and the population in 1900 was one hundred.

In the Russell, Toomsuba and Thompson area, the surnames recorded in 1841 were Brown, Russell, Clayton, Henderson, Killingsworth, Agnew and Lambert. Earlier settlers in the Toomsuba area around 1832 were Jim Keeton, Ephraim Odum, Neill McLaurin, Duncan Kelly, J. Clinton, Crosby Miller, John Calhoun, John Pierce and S.H. Shannon. Other family names were Griffith, Carr, Durr and McNeal. Through these communities ran Brandon Branch, Nanabe Creek, Possum Creek and Sucatolba Creek. The

Russell community was founded by John Russell six miles east of Meridian on the Alabama Great Southern Railroad. The post office was established on February 5, 1867. The population in 1900 was 40. Toomsuba is on the creek of the same name, located about five miles east of Russell. Originally Toomsuba was called McLaurin and, after the railroad (the Alabama Great Southern) arrived, McLaurin Station. *Toomsuba* is Indian for "Tomb of a Dead Horse." Its population in 1900 was 175.

In Kewanee, records reveal that the surnames of 1841 settlers were Smith, Clinton, Bynum, Lewis and Martin. Major settlements didn't happen until after 1846. Through these communities ran Toomsuba and Sucatolba Creeks. Kewanee is fourteen miles northeast of Meridian and was home to Choctaw chief Pushmataha. Here in 1836, J.R Browell constructed the first sawmill in the county. The first post office was established on October 18, 1866, with Matthais Riffle as postmaster.

Graham and Meehan were settled by the Adams, Fowler, Gilbert, Jones and Moffett families. These areas were sparsely settled, even in the late 1800s. Waterways that quenched the land were Tallahatta Creek, Bogue Flower Creek, Chunky River, Statinea Bogue Creek, Cow Creek and Rock

Simmons-Wright General Store, Kewanee. Built by William Simmons and Tom Wright, the store has operated since 1884. The original wooden structure burned down in 1926 and was reconstructed with brick that same year. *June Davidson collection.*

Sign for Complete, Mississippi. *Author's collection.*

Creek. Meehan was located approximately seven miles west of Meridian at the junction of the Alabama & Vicksburg (A&V) Railroad and the Tallahatta Railway, running north to Battlefield in Newton County. The post office was established on February 26, 1889, under the name of Siding. Willie Graham was postmaster. On October 31, 1902, the post office name was changed to Meehan Junction and was incorporated in 1906.

In Complete, Lost Gap and Savannah Grove, the early surnames were Jones, Russell, Fountaine, Daniel, Turner, Sikes, Dyass, Tabb, Loper, Graham, Dearman, Goodson, Lang, Bishop, Whitehead and Stafford. In 1860, Richard McLemore had land around today's St. Patrick and Rose Hill Cemeteries. In 1860, John Ball owned land in the Complete vicinity. Creeks were Burwell Creek, Hognose Creek, Loper Creek, Sowashee Creek, Brothers Creek, Gallagher Creek and Okatibbee Creek. Complete became a part of Meridian, and its post office was opened in 1896. Lost Gap, located three miles west of Meridian, was a railroad flag stop established in 1890. The mineral deposits in this area affected the magnetic needles of the compasses used by surveyors of the railroad. Savannah Grove was a community on both sides of the A&V Railroad at the junction of the A&V and the Gulf, Mobile & Northern (GM&N, which in 1940 merged with the Mobile & Ohio), known first as the Alabama & Vicksburg Junction. It later became Savannah Grove.

In Vimville, Warbington and Russell, most settlements were after 1846, primarily in the 1850s. Charles Rushing settled this area in 1860. Waterways are Nanabe Creek, Curtis Branch, Buckatunna Creek, Walker's Branch, Tedder Branch, Little Alamuchee Creek and Alamuchee Creek.

The Alamucha area was settled early on by the Hathorn, Rodgers, Rhodes, McCraney, Halton, Runnels, Holland, Wiggins, O'Neal and Marsh families. Little Alamuchee Creek, Alamuchee Creek and Salem Creek were the waterways. Alamucha, approximately fifteen miles northeast of Meridian, was the Indian village known as Old Town. Its post office was formed on November 11, 1840.

In southwest Lauderdale County near current Pine Forest Road and also in the Dunn's Falls area, early settlers were the Kelley, Grice, Haley, Arrant, Dear, Dyass, Riley, Jones, Stuckey, King, Hollimon, Arrington and Lang families. Most settlements occurred in late '40s and after. Chunky River, Tallahatta Creek, Possum Creek, Wanita Creek and Allen Creek are the waterways.

In Arundel and Savoy, the early settlers were the Sterling, Cooper, Grant, Carye, Jemison, Nicholas, Tabb, Carson, Vaughn (Pinkney), Bynum, Laney and Parker families. Waterways included Little Creek, Brown's Creek, Sowashee Creek, Okatibbee Creek, Hognose Creek, Graham Mill Creek and Coats Creek. Arundel was settled in 1853 and located six miles southwest of Meridian; it was also known as Arundel Springs. Dunn's Falls was settled in 1854 by John C. Dunn, who erected a sawmill, gristmill and hat factory.

The communities of Enzor, Pleasant Hill, Stinson, Wolf Springs and Zero had the surnames James, Martin, Hyde, Crosby, Wingate, Fisher and McInnis as early settlers in 1841. In 1850, Richard McLemore also had land in Sections 23 and 26. The waterways are Dry Creek and Long Creek. Zero, located six miles southeast of Meridian, was first known as Pleasant Hill community. The population in 1900 was fifty.

In the Increase vicinity, we find the surnames of McInnis, Wheat and Martin. This area was sparsely populated, and the waterways are Buckatunna

Creek, Tedder Branch, Brown's Creek, Little Brown's Creek, Bean Creek and Long Branch.

The communities of Collinsville and Martin were settled by the House, Bailes, Watters, Tutt and Worbington families in 1841. The waterways are Gin Creek and Mayatte Creek. Collinsville is located about fourteen miles north of Meridian. Nathaniel Monroe Collins owned a plantation, cotton gin and store here in 1867. Its post office was established on May 23, 1884, by M.M. Collins, father of U.S. congressman Ross Collins. Ross Collins married Alfreda Grant, daughter of timber magnate M.R. Grant.

In 1841, early names in Obadiah and Shucktown were the Watters, Huttan, Adair, Snowden, Coleman, Thompson, Davis, Shumate, Brooke and Weir families. Waterways included House, Hodge Branch, Okatibbee, Chickasawhay, Tompeat, Bales, White Branch, Rogers, Bailey and Bailey Branch Creeks. Obadiah, fourteen miles northeast of Meridian, established its post office on June 30, 1900, with Obadiah S. Ratcliff as postmaster.

Daleville and Lizelia's 1841 settlers were Hubbard, Lacy, Shumate, Smith, Dawkins, McKellar, Steed and Gorman. Running through the land were the Mosley Branch, Baker Creek, Ponta Creek, Bailey Creek, Wright Creek, Lost Horse Creek and Wildhorse Creek. Daleville, located north of Meridian, is three or four miles from the northern boundary of Lauderdale County. Settled in the early 1800s by Sam Dale, Daleville was home to the Cooper Institute, an important school in the 1800s. Lizelia, thirteen miles north of Meridian, is situated on Ponta Creek. Its population in 1900 was forty-eight, and it was first known as Daleville.

Early settlements of Lauderdale and Lockhart were the Flewellens (1840), Odoms, Coopwoods and Barefoots and the Holderness, Delk, Sigris and Harlin families. Waterways were Segars Creek, Wright Creek, Ponta Creek, Lost Horse Creek, Big Reed Creek, Possum Creek and Little Reed Creek. Lockhart, twelve miles northeast of Meridian, was on the Mobile & Ohio Railroad and had a Male and Female Institute. The population in 1900 was thirty. Its post office was established in 1866, and John S. Harvey was postmaster.

The Lauderdale Springs area in 1841 had the Griffin, Boyd, Hanna, Tuton, Hudon, Bevill, Gaylie, Houston, Coopwood, Warren, Edwards, Griffin, Delk, Watts, McCown, Green, Stanton, Allen and Beeson families. Waterways included Roasted Hog Creek and Ponta Creek.

The 1841 settlers of Bonita and Meridian included Lang, Crory, McLemore (Richard), Evens, Creal, Wood, Odom, Hall, Scarborough, Gordon, Deen, Newsom, Irby, Tims, Bishop, Morris, Dearman, Bozone, Stafford, Berrien (1840), Alexander, Clinton, Fairchild, Jones, Petagrew, Hill, Garrett, Pace and Warbington. Waterways were Magnolia Creek, Sowashee Creek, Brothers Branch Creek and Clear Creek. Bonita was settled around 1833 and established around 1896. In the 1900s, there was a large brickyard, oil mill and ice factory here.

Lauderdale, originally known as Springs Depot, is one of the oldest settlements in the county and is located approximately twenty miles northeast of Meridian. The post office for Springs Depot was established in the 1850s, and the name was changed to Lauderdale in 1894. The post office of Mingo Houma (Lauderdale Springs) was established on April 1, 1837, with Thomas H. Davis as postmaster.

History can't neglect the first black settlers, though most remain unnamed and their histories a mystery. But *Citizens of Color*, written, produced and published by John Barksdale, recorded Lauderdale County's black history as follows: "We see [the Negroes] clearing the swamps and forests, laying the railroad, cultivating the fields and toiling manually in every conceivable chore, with each succeeding generation rendering humanitarian services."

Other settlements and the dates their post offices opened include:

ARKLET: Formed in 1883 as a flag station outside Meridian, it was originally known as McInnis Crossing.

BATTLEFIELD: Located twenty miles southwest of Meridian, actually in the northeastern corner of Newton County, on Tallahatta Creek and the northern terminus of the Tallahatta Railroad running north from Meehan Junction on the A&V Railroad. Its post office was established on October 9, 1849, and its postmaster was James M. Trussell.

BIGGERS: Part of South Meridian, its post office was established on May 15, 1907, with Richard R. Biggers as postmaster.

BOZEMAN: Eight miles northwest of Meridian, its post office was opened on May 3, 1893, with Dora Bozeman as postmistress.

BRUNSON: A part of south Meridian, its post office was established on July 19, 1893, and Martha Yarbrough was postmistress.

BULLARDS: Located on the spur track of the M&O Railroad approximately eight miles southwest of Meridian.

Causeyville Store. Built in 1896, the store was placed on the National Register of Historic Places in 1986. *Author's collection.*

Bunnie: Located approximately nine miles north of Meridian, its post office was established on August 25, 1890. Ramson S. Richardson was postmaster.

Buttercup: Originated in 1885, it was located six miles north of Meridian. It later came to be known as Jackson Springs

Causeyville: Located about twelve miles southeast of Meridian, it was settled around 1884. Because there was already a "Causeyville" post office in Mississippi, the post office was established on January 5, 1887, and named "Edbony." This post office was abolished, and in 1894, a new post office named "Increase" was created in 1894, with W.J. Anderson as postmaster. In 1900, Increase had a population of fifty-three. In 1929, when the Increase Post Office was discontinued, the community became known again as Causeyville.

Celie: Begun in 1900 approximately eighteen miles southeast of Meridian, its post office was established on December 30, 1904. Floyd C. Hagwood was postmaster.

Chunkeyville: Located near the Newton County line west of Meridian on the A&V Railroad, its post office was established in 1848, and John G. Gallaspy was postmaster.

Cliff Williams: Located five miles southeast of Meridian.

Coonville: Located six miles northwest of Lauderdale, it was named in 1893 for a principal farmer by the name of "Coon" Clay. Coonville has been extinct since 1905.

COOSHA (KOONSHA) TOWN: Located two miles west of Lockhart on the route of the Tennessee Trade Road, or the "Big Trading Path."

DAHLGREEN: Established in 1868 approximately eighteen miles from Meridian in northwestern Lauderdale County.

DARNELL: Called Darnell Spur, it was located twelve miles southwest of Meridian on the A&V Railroad below Meehan. A sawmill was erected there in 1908.

EASTVILLE: Located four miles south of Meridian, its post office was established on December 8, 1891.

ENJOR: Located around six miles northeast of Meridian, its post office was established on April 23, 1902.

FORT STEPHENS: Located fourteen miles northwest of Meridian, in 1880, the southern part of the community became known as Shucktown. In 1903, when the post was established in Jim Snowden's store, the community became officially known as Snowden. Later, the southern part of this community became known as Center Hill.

FREEMAN: Located eight miles northwest of Meridian, its post office was established on May 28, 1901.

GILEAD: Settled in 1830 and located six miles northeast of Meridian, its post office was secured in 1895 and was named after the Baptist church. Thomas G. Pigford was postmaster.

GRAHAM: Settled in the 1880s by W.J. Graham, who built a large sawmill there, Graham is located about nine miles west of Meridian.

HAMMEL: This was a flag stop established in 1912 about seven miles northwest of Meridian.

HURRLA PLACE: Located about ten miles west of Meridian, the post office was secured on March 25, 1890.

LEEVILLE: Located two miles east of Battlefield at the terminus of the Tallahatta Railway spur, the post office was established on March 2, 1896, and Mattie Lee served as postmistress.

LISK: Located about twenty miles southeast of Meridian, its post office operated from 1866 until 1877, with L.S. McDonald as postmaster.

LODGE: Known as the Sand Flat Community in 1899, it was located in southeast Meridian. After a black man, E.L. Young, helped secure the Masonic Lodge Hall on the north side of Mt. Zion Church, the name of the community was changed to Lodge. The Lodge Post Office was opened on April 15, 1911. Spinks Jones served as postmaster. In 1918, the City of Meridian bought this land.

Magnolia: Eight miles northeast of Meridian, it was established in 1837. Its post office opened on April 20, 1839. Isaac Blair served as postmaster.

Markwell: This community is thought to have been located around the area of Marion. Its post office was opened on July 29, 1856. George W. Merrill served as postmaster.

Martin: Located twelve miles northwest of Meridian.

Mate: Located seven miles northwest at Didley Creek, this area was mostly a Negro settlement, and its post office was established on February 5, 1904. Thomas J. Shumate was postmaster.

Melwyn: Located five miles east of Meridian, in 1914 this area became known as Pigford because of the strawberry farm owned by J.A. and H.E. Pigford. The name was changed to Melwyn at the request of the Alabama Great Southern (AGS) Railroad.

Morrow: Located nine miles north of Meridian, the post office was established on September 12, 1890. William Joseph Morrow was postmaster. This area was later known as Andrew's Chapel.

Moseley: Twelve miles northwest of Meridian, between Suqualena and Schamberville, a siding and switch track was installed where J.T. Moseley operated his sawmill. This became known as Moseley's Crossing.

Okatibbee: Located seven miles south of Meridian and also known as Sterling, Okatibbee was a crossroads stop on the Mobile & Ohio (M&O) Railroad. On July 5, 1848, the post office opened as Sageville, with Martin C. Buxton as postmaster. Sometime after that, the name was changed to Okatibbee, but on April 7, 1857, the name was changed back to Sageville. On February 12, 1858, the name changed back to Okatibbee. In 1894, a new post office was secured with the name of Sterling.

Point: About twelve miles west of Meridian, Point was a flag stop on the Alabama & Vicksburg Railroad near Tunnel Hill. Its post office was established on September 17, 1895. Samuel H. Wilson was postmaster. The population in 1900 was twenty-seven.

Ponta: Located between Daleville and Vestals, Ponta was originally an Indian trading post. Located about fourteen miles north of Meridian, its post office opened on July 19, 1850, and William V. Raney was postmaster. The population in 1900 was thirty-six.

POST: Located eighteen miles northwest of Meridian, its post office was established on November 3, 1898, with John R. Rich as its first postmaster. Battlefield is the nearest railroad station. The population in 1900 was thirty.

RANSOM: Located ten miles east of Meridian and two miles east of Russell, the post office of Ransom was established on July 29, 1854. Charles Ransom was the postmaster.

RUSHING'S STORE: Located twelve miles northwest of Meridian on Okatibbee Creek, one mile south of Center Hill School, the post office was established on July 31, 1860, with Hampton L. Williamson as postmaster. The population in 1900 was forty.

SAMPSON: Located fifteen miles northeast of Meridian, the post office was established on February 1, 1873. Sampson later became a part of Lockhart.

SCHAMBERVILLE: Located twelve miles northwest of Meridian, it was named for Captain C.W. Schamber. Its post office was established on September 18, 1913.

SHOPS: Located at what are now Tenth Street and Thirty-eighth Avenue, Shops was established in 1926 and designed to handle railroad mail only.

SMITH: Located approximately fifteen miles from Meridian between Kewanee and Toomsuba, Smith was named for Ed Smith and was the location of Dixie High Consolidated School.

SMITH'S SPUR: Located northeast of Meridian two miles from Kewanee, the first post office in community was called Tonic. Then the name was changed to Blanks Station, after the Blanks family. Later, it was changed to Smith's Spur because the Smith family had been the earliest residents of the community.

Stinson: Located three miles south of Meridian, the post office was established on February 25, 1899. The postmaster was William H. Stinson

TEMPLE: Located on the old Jackson Trail three miles south of Daleville, the post office, which opened in 1895, was named for W.F. Temple, the first postmaster.

TISDALE: Located thirteen miles northeast of Meridian, its post office opened on March 27, 1901, and was named after its postmaster, John S. Tisdale.

TOPTON: Located about three miles southwest of Lockhart and six miles northeast of Meridian, it was a flag stop on the M&O Railroad in 1861. The post office was established on January 15, 1890.

TUNNEL HILL: The railroad came through this section in 1861, but the post office was not established until October 11, 1896, with its postmaster being Charles M. Doty.

A young lady waits patiently at the Topton Flag Station. *Courtesy of Lauderdale County Department of Archives and History.*

VESTALS: Named for George Vestal and located about fourteen miles northeast of Meridian, Vestals was a flag stop on the M&O Railroad.

WHYNOT: Old Whynot was located three miles north of its present site, which lies about nineteen miles southeast of Meridian. The post office was opened in 1887. The population in 1900 was thirty-two.

WILSONDALE: Two miles south of Collinsville, this was a Negro school community established around 1900. It was not named until the Memphis & Meridian Railroad was built through the community and then was named after Professor Thomas Jefferson Wilson. This Negro community had a privately owned race track.

WRIGHTS: About fifteen miles northeast of Meridian, this community was first known as Webb. The name changed when the Wright family settled in the area around 1860.

EARLY TRAVEL

Many early roads had been Indian trails that crisscrossed the county, such as the stage road through Daleville and Lauderdale Springs. Daleville was one of the first communities to have stagecoach service. Original surveys showed a road running southwest to northeast between Lauderdale and Enterprise, which is likely the early route of U.S. Highway 11. This road probably ran through present-day Meridian by way of Sixth Street. One mail and stage route was possibly the "Choctaw Trail." On this route was a stagecoach stop erected in 1800 in the community of Lauderdale. Other important roads of the time were the Marion–Livingston Road, as well as Gaston Road running from Marion to Alabama by way of Alamucha. An early road to Alabama probably followed the route of Highway 19 through Lauderdale County. Decatur Road from Marion may have followed today's Seventh Street in Meridian.

A major stage line during the antebellum days was the Jemison and Ficklin stage line. Its coaches arrived in Marion on Monday, Wednesday and Friday evenings, stopping at the Bains Hotel located in the town square, where passengers enjoyed a meal in the hotel's café.

Every year, settlers participated in the maintenance of early roads by offering free labor. The map of 1868 reveals a road from Marion to Alamucha, which curved and descended south of Toomsuba. As it continued north to Alamucha, it forked. The right fork led into the Old Whynot area and on into the old Tuscumbia Road to Antioch. The fairly straight road from Alamucha to Old Whynot most likely followed a ridge close to the Old Marion–Alamucha Road after the Marion–Alamucha Road curved northward. According to the *History of Whynot*, Isaiah Gardner was overseer of the road in 1847 and D.C. Wallace in 1848.

The map of 1855 revealed the road from Old Marion, which ran east of the Sand Flats area and past old Bolen's Store on Highway 19E to Quitman in Clarke County. Another road ran from Hurricane (Creek) southwest to Quitman. The road known as the Mobile Road, which was an old Indian path, ran from Marion to Whynot and crossed what is now Old Wire Road. Old Whynot was in the same area as the present-day Boy Scout Camp Binachi.

Various postal routes connected to stage routes, such as the one from Winchester to Daleville that had connections to Columbus and Jackson. In the 1840s, there were coaches from Tuscaloosa, Alabama, through Lauderdale Springs. Route 5763 went from Daleville to Marion, Quitman and Chickasawhay and into Winchester. Route 5702, from Jackson to Livingston, Alabama, went through Brandon, Sandy Hill, Hillsboro, County Line, Union, Herbert, Oktibbeha, Daleville and Mingo Houma (Lauderdale Springs).

EDUCATION ON THE FRONTIER

Somewhere around 1835, after their homes and a few churches had been built, families in proximity to one another banded together to establish a "patron" school, where one settler furnished a log cabin, another furnished wood and bare necessities (such as tables, chairs, etc.) and everyone pitched in to pay the teacher. The schoolhouse was usually located near a waterway, like a spring or creek, to ensure an ample water supply. Often, church services, community meetings and justice of the peace court were held in the school. When a new community church was built, sometimes the school relocated into the old church building.

Referred to as academies, such as White Sulfur Springs Academy in Lauderdale and Walnut Springs Academy in the Alamucha area, patron schools existed in or near Marion, Alamucha, Sageville, Bailey, Suqualena and Lauderdale. Grades one and two, for one or two four-month periods, were taught each year. Higher education academies were Marion Academy, established in 1837, and Alamucha, formed in 1838. Later academies were Pinckney-Vaughn Academy and the Cook Academy.

On May 9, 1837, an act was passed to incorporate the first trustees of the Marion Academy. They were James Ruton, James Murray, Benjamin T. Larke, John R. Leath, Isaac Barr, John F. Chester, Horatio B. Warbington and Theodore S. Swift. Trustees were empowered to receive donations and purchase or mortgage real estate, purchases not to exceed $5,000 and personal estate not to exceed $10,000. Another stipulation was that the academy could not be located more than one mile from Marion.

The Board of Police, formed by the laws of the State of Mississippi in 1841, had varied duties, such as lending money for the improvement of roads and bridges, assigning road workers and accepting bids for the construction of bridges. The board also established guidelines for the state's public school system, including the appointment of a school commissioner for each district. It divided each respective county into five districts. From each district, qualified voters elected one member for the term prescribed in the constitution under the rules and regulations the board had adopted. The first members of the Board of Police served for a period of eighteen months until the second election, which was for a period of two years.

The first five districts were set up in April 1834, but there are no records because, in November 1837, they were burned in the courthouse fire at Old Marion. On November 16, 1847, the Lauderdale County Board of Police consisted of L.B. Banes (Bains), president; Isaac G. Suttles; L.B. Moore; Daniel Cameron; and A. (Abie) Clay.

BUSINESS

As cotton prosperity thrived in the mid-1830s, more and more forests were sacrificed for fields. Though production of cotton greatly improved and increased, corn remained the principal staple in the South throughout the antebellum period. Easily grown all over Mississippi, corn was an important food crop to everyone, including hogs, cattle and other livestock. The long growing season allowed for two crops of corn to be planted each year, one in early March and the other in late May or June. Cottonseed was used as a fertilizer, and cowpeas were planted between the rows of corn to reduce erosion and to add nitrogen to improve the soil's fertility.

Thousands of immigrants, planters, farmers and speculators had poured into Mississippi for the abundant cheap land, lenient credit requirements and high prices for crops. More banks had been established and were issuing notes with no regard for solvency. State government was hoarding gold and silver, using instead paper notes to discharge debts. In 1837, President Martin van Buren stepped into a new administration and a major bank crisis. People in Lauderdale County who invested in failing banks like Brandon Bank and Mississippi Union Bank included Norman and Ann Martin, Neil and Jane McLaurin and James Keeton; their investments included mortgaging homes, land and even slaves. On September 6, 1847, real estate assets of the Mississippi Union Bank in Lauderdale County were auctioned at the courthouse in Marion.

The 1840 census showed that Lauderdale County had produced 20,000 pounds of cotton, as compared to 193,402,577 in the state, with dairy products valued at $336 and homemade and family goods valued at $3,622. There were two businesses under "retail dry goods, grocery and other stores" and one tannery with an investment of $350, compared to 128 in the state. There were 37 men employed in oil mills (presumably cotton), with 81,000 invested in the industry, compared to 923 men and an investment of 1,219,845 in the state. There were also 10 gristmills (805 in the state) and 12 sawmills (309 in the state).

Gristmills were common implements because corn was ground into meal. Cornbread was much more common than wheat bread. There were only 4 brick and stone houses but 256 wooden houses. There were 527 men employed in house building. Lauderdale County lacked large rivers, but there were enough waterways that, if dammed, produced enough water power to turn a mill's waterwheel. Because operating a mill, whether a gristmill or sawmill, required serious alterations to the natural landscape and the waterways had to be dammed, the law required that operations be licensed and controlled. Early mills included Beason's mill on Nanabe Creek near Sageville, Rigsby Mills, Lauderdale Springs and Davis Mill on Decatur Road.

At a spot where the Chunky River flowed less than one hundred yards from a high bluff in southwest Lauderdale County, Irish immigrant John C. Dunn bought the land and constructed a dam to divert the flow of the river

Stuckey Bridge, South Lauderdale County. *Author's collection.*

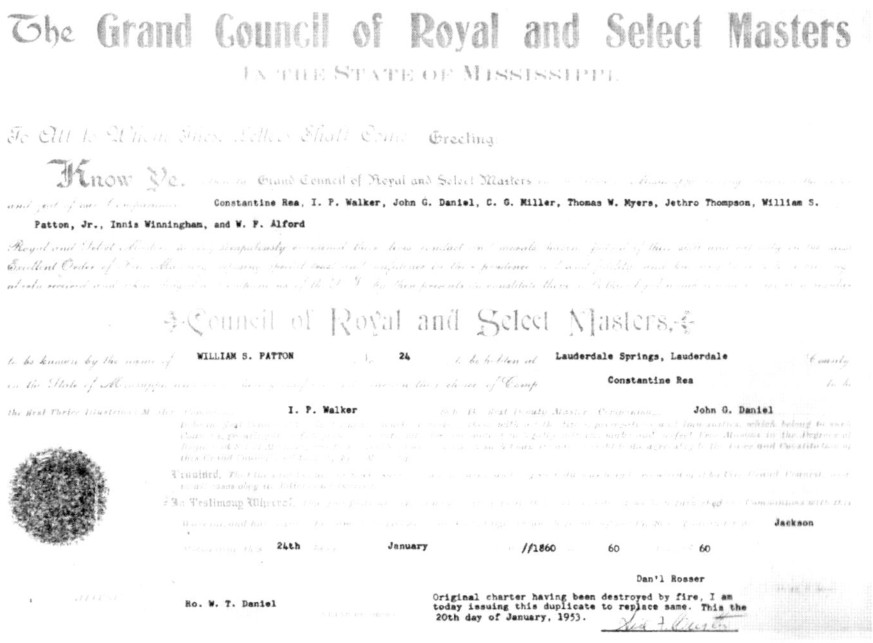
The Grand Council of Royal and Select Masters
IN THE STATE OF MISSISSIPPI.

Greeting

Know Ye. Grand Council of Royal and Select Masters

Constantine Rea, I. P. Walker, John G. Daniel, C. G. Miller, Thomas W. Myers, Jethro Thompson, William S. Patton, Jr., Innis Winningham, and W. F. Alford

Council of Royal and Select Masters,

WILLIAM S. PATTON 24 Lauderdale Springs, Lauderdale

Constantine Rea

I. P. Walker John G. Daniel

Jackson

24th January //1860 60 60

Dan'l Rosser

Ro. W. T. Daniel

Original charter having been destroyed by fire, I am today issuing this duplicate to replace same. This the 20th day of January, 1953.

Certificate for the Con Rea Grand Masters. *Courtesy of Lauderdale County Department of Archives and History.*

over the bluff. This produced a sixty-five-foot waterfall that supplied water power for his mill. He also created a millpond to store water, which allowed the mill a constant, controllable source of power. By 1860, he was operating a ceramic plant using the clay from the hills in the area. The falls powered a lumber mill and a three-story cotton gin. Dunn and his buildings and machinery would become crucial to the later Confederate war effort.

Other Lauderdale County businesses were Tempy Store on the Alamucha–Whynot Road, owned by a black woman known as Aunt Tempy, and the Booker store in downtown Whynot, first owned by B.P. "Brick" Means and designated as the area's voting location.

Born in Maury County, Tennessee, in 1825, Con Rea settled in Marion in the mid-1840s with his wife, Margaret, and their first child, Richard Nathan Rea. Rea practiced law in Lauderdale, Kemper, Neshoba, Newton, Jasper and Clark Counties in Mississippi and in Alabama's Sumter and Choctaw Counties. In January 1854, Rea and Charles Wesley Henderson purchased an interest in the *Lauderdale Republican* newspaper, founded by William Penn Andrews around 1851.

The *Lauderdale Republican* recorded many newsworthy items and the breaking news of business activities. In some of these issues we learn that D.U. Ford was a physician and surgeon in Marion; W.P. Evans was a Marion attorney; bids were being taken on Alamucha Academy, Marion, evidencing the school's longevity; D.U. Ford helped settle a dispute between Con Rea and Harper and Bains; and the Eagle tin shop was established in Marion by James A. Radcliffe, opposite Semmes' Blacksmith Shop on the east side of the public square. "Robinson and Eldred's Circus" was to be held in Marion on May 4, 1854. A camp meeting would be held at the campground five miles northwest of Marion. L.B. Bains, president of Marion Male Academy, had purchased Planters and Railroad Hotel from Walter W. Welch and changed the name to the Bains' Hotel. Concerts were given by concert flutist Madame Siminski, with Miss Reynolds singing and playing violin, guitar, flute and piano. The Riley family musicians gave concerts at the courthouse on violin, cello and guitar. The newspaper reported that a few in the audience had been boisterous. Traveling artist B.T. Freeman was in Marion for a while and stayed above Burton's Saddle Shop on the north side of the square.

We learn that a band of Choctaws passed through Marion on their way to the Indian Territory, W.C. Calhoun had for sale a likely Negro fellow and there would be a sheriff's sale of slaves belonging to Rebecca Tucker to satisfy claims of Samuel Lehman. We also learn that a Negro woman hanged herself at the residence of John Crane.

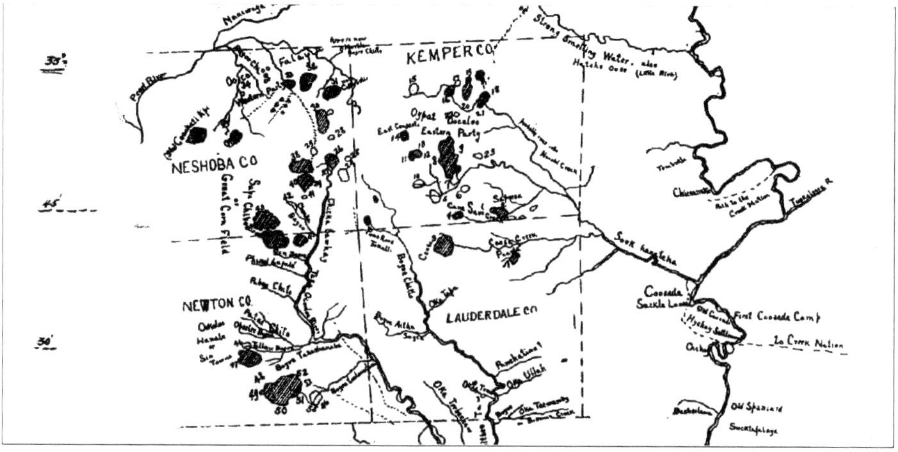

1855 Lauderdale County map. *Mississippi Department of Archives and History.*

Frontier life was difficult. But life for slaves was arduous and in vain since slaves had no rights to their lives, their families or any land upon which they toiled. The *Plantation Diary of H. Blackwood*, overseer of the B.F. Moore Plantation located in the southwest corner of Lauderdale County near present-day Arundel, best describes the endless, exhaustive days of plantation work for the slaves and the Irish workers who ditched the land.

Each day, Blackwood recounted the daily tasks of the slaves and workers. On January 25, 1859, signs of rain began. Blackwood reported that the Irishman, Cooney, commenced ditching for B.F. Moore on January 26, 1859. From here, as the hard rains came, the number of sick began to increase:

> *Thursday, Jan. 27, 1859. Blake rolled logs and cleaned up trash with 17 of the women, boys, and chaps, seven of the men cut logs, three ditched, three worked on a chimney until about 11 o'clock. Then all business stopped on account of heavy raining, then some shelled corn, the women sode* [sewed] *for themselves and children, eight sick, Jery, Poley, July, Froney, Jenney, Freybo, Albert and Axom. Continued to rain study* [steady]. *Cooney ditched until 10 o'clock and the rain stopped him for the balance of the day.*

Friday's count for the sick was at eight, and on Saturday Blackwood reported that the plantation was full of water because of the rains. Some daily tasks for the slaves were rolling logs, hauling and burning logs, cleaning brush, ditching, plowing and hauling manure. Ditching and trenching were to try to drain the water from the fields so they could prepare them for planting. Reports of the sick revealed chills and fever. The heavy rains continued, as did the slave labor of rolling logs, plowing, ditching, cutting timber and splitting rails to fix fences. On Thursday, February 17, Blackwood reported that the ground was so wet he could not plow at all:

> *Monday, Feb. 21, 1859. Blacke and the women burned logs and cleaned up. Jef and eight of the boys trenched land to drain the water off to get it dry enough to plow. Six plowed, 5 double plows, one single, four ditched, two split palings, Jim worked some in garden. Melton made plow stocks. Parley sick. Barbery sick. Charity guntin* [grunting] *and not much the matter. Coney ditched all day today for B.F. Moore.*

> *WEDNESDAY, FEB. 23, 1859. Blake and the women, boys and chaps burned logs and cleaned up trash in general in the swamp field. Seven plowed, five double plows and two single plows. Four ditched. Three of the boys split rales. Jef fixed bridges. Abram—he ditches until night. Jim sow some seed in the garden then went to work about his hogs. Melton made plow stocks. Poley, Barby, Hary sick. We have more rain today. We plowed today in the March field. Coney ditched all day today for B.F. Moore.*

The rains continued into March. The sick included Poley, Barbery, Hary, Mary, Amey, Ann and Patsy. Harrit miscarried on Saturday, February 26, 1859. Sunday was the day of rest. Blackwood recorded that Harrit was sick on Monday but not on Tuesday, indicating that she had returned to work. On March 3, it was recorded that "the field seemed to be a pond of water," and the rains continued—as did the labor. Amey, one of the sick listed, died from pneumonia on March 15. Dr. More and Dr. Chackleford attended her. Hery and Alfred dug her grave on March 16. Amey was listed in the diary as Milton's wife. On March 18, Axom was sick with pneumonia. On March 19, it was recorded that no plowing had been done for nine days due to the land being so wet. On April 14, collard plants were planted, and on April 16, "Jef and Dock went for a load of cotton seed." On April 18, cotton land was bedded, and corn land in the oat patch field was rebedded. On April 19, nine plows planted corn, and six rebedded corn land. On April 21, they finished planting oat patch corn. Jef hauled cottonseed to plant cotton the next day. The seed was recorded as "shearrod" cottonseed. Planting cotton commenced on April 22 and continued until May 12. On May 13, they broke up a potato patch and went to plowing and replanting corn.

Hoeing and chopping cotton commenced around this time in May. By June, the weather had changed to hot and dry, and Blackwood recorded:

> *THURSDAY, JUNE 2, 1859. All business going on today as yesterday and no change at all only Melton is at work on a wagon body. Jim working in the garden. Sick the same. The weather hot and dry. We need rain very bad. The corn on the Block land looks like it will die soon if it don't rain. The cotton looks too like it will die.*

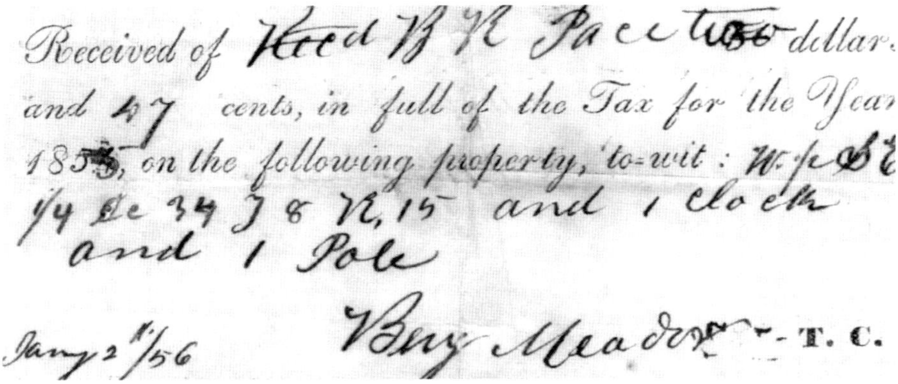

Received of Hood B R Pace two dollars and 47 cents, in full of the Tax for the Year 1855, on the following property, to-wit: W ½ SE ¼ Sec 34 T 8 R 15 and 1 Clock and 1 Pole

Jany 21/56 Benj Meador - T. C.

Tax receipt, 1856. *Courtesy of Lauderdale County Department of Archives and History.*

Cotton was hoed throughout the summer until picking time in August, the hottest time of year in Mississippi.

Cane molasses, now a southern staple, was almost unknown in antebellum days. Most likely, the immigrants from the eastern states introduced tobacco growing. Records reveal that 1,529 pounds of tobacco were produced in 1850, as compared to 170 pounds in 1860, indicating that the land probably wasn't suitable for growing tobacco.

In 1858, farmers of Lauderdale County formed the Agricultural and Mechanical Society of Lauderdale County, which sponsored a fair at Marion Station. Men, women and children entered their best products for judging. Some results were as follows:

AGRICULTURAL PRODUCTS

W.J. Brown, most cotton produced on five acres, $10

C.E. Rushing, one hundred pounds of the best grade of hay, $3

Reverend W.C. Emerson, one bottle of "Chinese syrup," $3

GARDEN CROPS

C.E. Rushing, one dozen of the largest and finest turnips, $2

Thomas L. Jackson, largest and best beet, $2

Mrs. Ann J. McElroy, largest and best pie melon, $2

Stock

L.M. Chandler, best two-year-old "common" colt, $3

James F. Tinnon, best two-year-old mule colt, $2

Poultry

Mrs. A.L. Burwell, finest rooster, $1

Prizes were also given for "Dairy and Household," "Manufacture of Leather," "Domestic Manufacture," "Fancy Work" and "Workshop."

The 1850 census records for Lauderdale County reveal a white population of 6,052 and a slave population of 2,661. The 1850 agriculture census indicated the following annual statistics for the year ending June 1, 1850:

Acres of improved land: 51,386
Acres of unimproved land: 86,714
Livestock: horses–2,080
asses and mules–418
milch cows–4,839
working oxen–1,695
other cattle–6,580
sheep–6,191
swine–28,481
Bushels of wheat: 2,808
Bushels of rye: 109
Bushels of Indian corn: 324,459
Bushels of oats: 21,771
Pounds of rice: 102,203
Pounds of tobacco: 1,529
Bales of cotton (400 pounds each): 4,195
Pounds of wool: 10,500
Bushels of peas and beans: 15,411
Bushels of Irish potatoes: 3,705
Bushels of sweet potatoes: 111,444
Bushels of barley: 20
Bushels of buckwheat: 150
Pounds of butter: 69,034

Pounds of cheese: 888
Toss of hay: 10
Pounds of hop: 20
Pounds of beeswax honey: 20,344

In 1860, corn remained the major staple crop in Lauderdale County, enjoying an increase in production of approximately 46 to 47 percent. However, from 1850 to 1860, the county's cotton production rose by astonishing amounts, with an enormous increase of approximately 370 percent.

RELIGION AND SOCIAL TIME

From 1817 to 1860, religion expanded, with most early churches on preaching circuits. The largest denominations in Lauderdale County were Baptist and Methodist. The Mississippi Baptist Association, formed in 1806, witnessed the pulling away of several churches, which formed the Union Association in 1819. The next year, other Baptist groups formed the Pearl River Association. Some were divided on the question of missionary work, while some believed it was God's duty to convert the heathen. Many refused to join the State Convention, which had been organized at Clear Creek Church in Washington. More divisions happened in the Baptist denomination than in any other. Disputes were over doctrine and matters such as the use of instruments in church, as well as the controversial issue of Freemasonry.

This period ushered in the camp meeting, known now as the revival. Temperance societies fought against sinful vices. In 1854, the Mississippi legislature passed a local measure forbidding retail liquor in any police town or district, unless approved by a majority vote.

By 1860, the Methodist denomination had the largest number of churches in the state of Mississippi. The Baptist denomination had the largest number of members. Churches became the center of family life, prohibiting unbecoming behavior, such as drinking whiskey, gambling, fighting, dancing, fiddling or doing business on Sundays, even bartering livestock. Allowing stock to trespass on a neighbor's property was an offense in the church's eye.

Sageville Methodist Church, founded in the early 1830s. *Author's collection.*

If a church member violated one of these rules, he or she might have to face the congregation to defend the accusation or ask forgiveness for the "sin." If the church didn't pardon the wrongdoing, said member could be expelled from the church and face public disgrace.

Long before the Treaty of Dancing Rabbit Creek, Presbyterian and Catholic missionaries had worked among the Choctaws. The Presbyterian Church, established in Lauderdale County in 1856, had John T. Ball and Lewis Andrews Ragsdale serving as elders. That same year, the first Episcopal Church service was conducted by Bishop William Mercer Green. Catholic missionaries were sent into Lauderdale County in the mid-1800s, but the growth of the Catholic faith didn't happen until later.

Marion grew politically, economically and socially as the county seat. The mid-1850s welcomed the Mobile & Ohio Railroad, and the town offered a livery stable complete with buggies, hacks and horses for hire. Concerts and cotillion parties held at the Mansion House roused the atmosphere with lively entertainment. West of the square, square dances were held in

Toomsuba Presbyterian Church, founded 1836. *Author's collection.*

the big gray barn. Outside the village, bets were placed at the horse track. Along the square, women shopped at Harper and Bains and purchased from the Ragland and Company Drugstore medicinal products, such as Jacob's Cordial, morphine and even fine brandy and Spanish cigars. The billiard hall with card tables and the tavern were always packed. Close to election time, political rallies lured large crowds from miles around, and festivities included feasting, drinking and horse racing. Travelers checked into hotels, where they dined before going out for entertainment. If the Bains Hotel proved to be too pricey, there was the less expensive Preston House at Old Marion.

In the mid-1800s, Lauderdale Springs resort, then under the management of B.B. Smith, had a two-story hotel, cottages, bathhouses and a dance pavilion. The resort provided a first-class stage line that ferried guests to and from the hotel to Lauderdale and Marion Stations. The spur line also ran from Spring Depot at Lauderdale to the resort.

THE RAILROAD

On September 20, 1850, Congress donated land to Alabama and Mississippi to assist in the construction of the Mobile & Ohio (M&O) Railroad. Con Rea had predicted that Marion would be the primary beneficiary. But southwest of Marion was a village known to most as McLemore's Old Field, named after the first settler of the area, Richard McLemore.

Alabamian L.A. Ragsdale had heard that the M&O and the Southern would cross somewhere close to the McLemore Plantation. According to *Lauderdale County: The Early Years*, Ragsdale purchased land from McLemore on September 22, 1853, and ran his tavern from McLemore's first home. John T. Ball bought approximately eighty acres from McLemore and built his store on the corner of the current Twenty-sixth Avenue and Seventh Street, known then as Lower Decatur Road. This road (Seventh Street) branched off from the Enterprise Road (now known as Sixth Street). On June 20, 1854, Ball opened a post office under the name of "Meridian," with Alfred Beck as postmaster.

On November 6, 1854, Ragsdale bought an additional four hundred acres from McLemore, Elizabeth Creel, William P. Dodd, Ferdinand and Martha Snow and Harris T. and Eliza Jane Dearman. Most of Ragsdale's holdings were located in the center of the county.

By September 4, 1855, the M&O had reached Grimes Depot, about nine miles south of Meridian. The first scheduled train arrived at John Ball's rustic train station, Sowashee, on October 29, 1855.

Stamps off an L.A. Ragsdale deed. *Courtesy of Lauderdale County Department of Archives and History.*

Granted by Congress were railroad right of ways that might be twelve to thirty miles wide, making the M&O a large landowner in Lauderdale County. The M&O sold much of this land at prices four times greater than the price of public land. In June 1857, it sold twelve hundred acres at land auctions held at Lauderdale Springs and Marion Station. On June 15 and 16, 1858, Ragsdale offered five hundred lots for sale at public outcry in the "City of Ragsdale," alias "Meridian," evidencing his belief that he was the founder of this growing town.

The Southern Railroad headed east in 1859. Originally, the line was set for Enterprise, a thriving community in Clarke County. When its residents rejected it, Ragsdale and Ball joined efforts to bring the Southern into their village by promising both land and assistance. After the deal was sealed, they publicized and promoted the coming of the Southern.

On February 10, 1860, the Mississippi legislature passed the following act:

> *Be it enacted by the Legislature of the State of Mississippi that all that piece, parcel or tract of country known as the whole of Section 18, township 6, Range 16, east and the west half of the N.W. quarter of Section 17, Township 6, Range 16, east be incorporated under the name and style of the city of Meridian.*

The new township extended from the current Thirty-first Avenue on the west, along Fourteenth Street on the north to Tenth Avenue on the east, to where B Street crosses around Seventeenth Avenue, and then along St. Andrews on the south back to Thirty-first Avenue, covering little more than one square mile. J.G. Gibbs was Meridian's first mayor, elected in 1859 before the incorporation.

SECESSION

The 1800 census showed a population of 5,300,000 Americans, including 1,000,000 blacks, of whom 90 percent were slaves. By 1810, the population had risen to 7,239,881, with the black population reaching 1,377,808. Of those, 186,746 were free. The Mississippi census of 1840 reported that there were 179,074 whites and 196,577 people of color for a total population of 375,651.

Marion was a prosperous town with a drugstore, a provision store, two saddle and harness shops, two blacksmith shops, six dry goods dealers, a carriage and wagon shop and a male academy and female academy. Two saddle factories, a carriage factory, a family grocery and a silversmith were being constructed. Immigrant peddlers came selling a vast array of merchandise, including horses, mules and slaves. The *Lauderdale Republican* recorded that on January 15, 1856, a peripatetic trader auctioned off twenty-six slaves here.

The nation's political arena fought zealously on both sides of the slavery question. The *Lauderdale Republican* praised Marion's pristine loveliness, healthfulness and the merry sound of the slave and the sickle.

In the community of Suqualena, Pinckney Vaughn owned a considerable plantation that consisted of approximately 675 acres, a residence, outbuildings, slave quarters and a cotton gin. In Alamucha, J.P. Welch's estate consisted of over 4,000 acres. Its two-story Colonial-style building had pillars extending to the upper porch and a parlor, a dining room, three bedrooms and a hall. Its rear porch separated the dining room from a bedroom. The kitchen, as was customary in those days, was detached but had a covered walkway. Each room had a fireplace. Around sixty slaves lived in the row of log cabins behind the house. Most of the family's food was produced on the estate, which also possessed a cotton gin and smithy. In Chunkeyville, the Stuckey family ran a 400-acre plantation. Other plantation owners were Colonel E.A. Durr, a Marion businessman, and Peter Bozeman, who settled in the Toomsuba area around 1840. Bozeman's slave quarters were located on the south side of his large residence. B.F. "Bart" Moore's plantation in the Sageville-Arundel area encompassed 3,500 acres, which required extra hands of the Irish immigrants who had fled Ireland's Potato Famine. W.E. Prince and George W. Chandler owned plantations in the Pine Springs area.

Theodore Kornweibel, professor of African American history, found documented evidence for slave labor on over 75 percent of southern railroads, estimating that over ten thousand slaves a year labored on the railroads in the South between 1857 and 1865. Before the Civil War, a contractor by the name of Scott and a number of slaves dug through the hills between Toomsuba and Russell for the railroad from Meridian to Selma.

Lauderdale County's farmland value had increased by 176 percent, and acreage increased by 50 percent. Businesses and industries flourished, with nine flour and gristmills, nine sawmills and four tanneries. In 1859, Mississippi led in the value of orchard produce and was fourth in livestock production. Agricultural bounties included Indian corn, sweet potatoes, rice and cotton. By 1860, the county's slave population had more than doubled.

Due to this prosperity, by 1860, many non–slave owners were buying slaves. Cotton production in the state of Mississippi was thirty times greater than in the '50s, and it provided one-fourth of the nation's cotton. According to *Mississippi: A History*, there was also substantial growth in livestock production and the production of rye, wheat, peas, tobacco, beans, Irish potatoes, corn, orchard and market garden products and wines.

With the election of President Abraham Lincoln in 1860, South Carolina seceded from the Union. The *Journal of the Mississippi Secession Convention, January 1861*, disclosed the following reasons for seceding from the Union:

> *Declaration of the Immediate Causes which Induce and Justify the Secession of the State of Mississippi from the Federal Union*
> *In the momentous step which our State has taken of dissolving its connection*

with the government of which we long formed a part, it is but just that we should declare the prominent reasons which have induced our course.

Our position is thoroughly identified with the institution of slavery—the greatest material interest of the world. Its labor supplies the product which constitutes by far the largest and most important portions of the commerce of the earth. These products are peculiar to the climate verging on the tropical regions, add by an imperious law of nature, none but the black race can bear exposure to the tropical sun. The products have become necessities of the world, and a blow at slavery is a blow at commerce and civilization. That blow has been long aimed at the institution, and was at the point of reaching its consummation. There was no choice left us but submission to the mandates of abolition, or a dissolution of the Union, whose principles had been subverted to work out our ruin.

The hostility to this institution commenced before the adoption of the Constitution and was manifested in the well-known Ordinance of 1787, in regard to the Northwestern Territory.

...It has grown until it denies the right of property in slaves, and refuses protection to what right on the high seas in the Territories and wherever the government of the United States has jurisdiction.

It refuses the admission of new slave States into the Union, and seeks to extinguish it by confining it within its presents limited, denying the power of expansion.

It tramples the original equality of the South under foot.

It has nullified the Fugitive Slave Law in almost every free State of the Union, and has utterly broken the compact which our fathers pledged their faith to maintain.

It advocates Negro equality, socially and politically, and promotes insurrection and incendiarism in our midst.

It has made combinations and formed associations to carry out its schemes of emancipation in the States and wherever else slavery exists.

It seeks not to elevate or to support the slave, but to destroy his present condition without providing a better way.

The Mississippi flag would be of "white ground, a Magnolia tree in the centre, a blue field in the upper left-hand corner with a white star in the centre, the flag to be finished with a red border and a red fringe at the extremity of the Flag."

Mississippi seceded from the Union on January 9, 1861.

THE CIVIL WAR

The Meridian Campaign

What followed secession was a war beyond all wars, friend against friend, brother against brother and father against son. Mary Lincoln's three brothers died fighting for the Confederacy. Varina Davis (Jefferson Davis's second wife) had relatives in the Union army. A nephew of Robert E. Lee commanded a Union squadron on the James River. The first shot of the Civil War was fired on April 12, 1861, at 4:30 a.m.

Lauderdale County volunteer units included the Lauderdale Rifles, Con Rea, captain; Lauderdale Zouaves, Kennon McElroy, captain; Alamucha Infantry, Peter H. Bozeman, captain; Pettus Guards, S.J. Randall, captain; Defenders, W.H. Hardy, captain; Lauderdale Spring Greys, B.B. Smith, captain; Walthall's Brigade, T.C. Carter, captain.

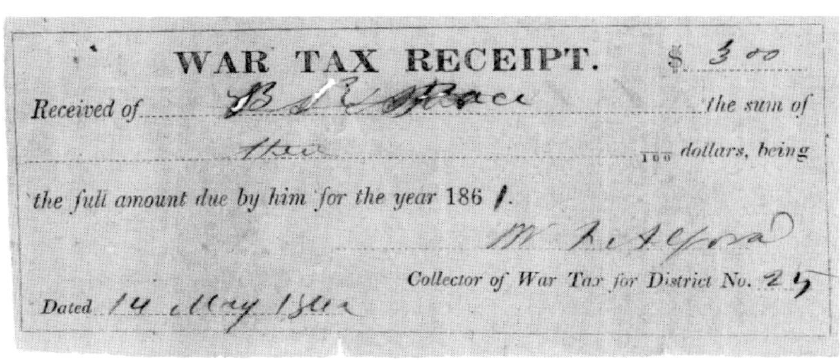
WAR TAX RECEIPT. $ 3 00

Received of B. S. E. ...ace *the sum of*

thee $\frac{}{100}$ *dollars, being*

the full amount due by him for the year 186 1.

Collector of War Tax for District No. 25

Dated 14 May 1861

War tax reciept, 1861. *Courtesy of Lauderdale County Department of Archives and History.*

These units formed the Thirteenth Mississippi Regiment, organized on May 14, 1861.

The long-anticipated Southern Railway locomotive Mazeppa pulled into Meridian on May 29, 1861. On board was a military company of 111 men from Vicksburg headed to training camp.

The Vicksburg Campaign was one of the most important campaigns of the war. The first attack on Vicksburg in the summer of 1862 and the second in late 1862 failed. Victory came only after General Ulysses S. Grant besieged the river town and starved its inhabitants. In the intense heat of July 4, 1863, Vicksburg surrendered.

Next, was the Meridian Campaign.

The writings of General William Tecumseh Sherman reveal his guilt in bringing his family into Mississippi, where son Willie had become sick and later died. On October 6, 1863, he wrote to his wife, Ellen:

> *Why, oh, why should this child be taken from us, leaving us full of trembling and reproaches? Though I know we did all human beings could do to arrest the ebbing tide of life, still I will always deplore my want of judgment in taking my family to so fatal a climate at so critical a period of the year… To it must be traced the loss of that child on whose future I had based all the ambition I ever had.*

Between the Vicksburg Campaign and the Meridian Campaign, Sherman's tactics escalated into his "total war" mindset.

The mill at Dunn's Falls had been used by the Confederacy to produce items such as blankets, clothing and hats. A distillery and blacksmith shop were added to aid in the war effort. The Lauderdale Springs Resort was now a hospital for Confederate soldiers, and the railroad spur that had been used to transport patrons to the Lauderdale Springs Resort was now used to deliver wounded Confederate soldiers to the hospital. According to *The Campaigns of Lieutenant General N.B. Forrest*, Nathan Bedford Forrest commented that this hospital was "admirably arranged and managed by Surgeon Thompson, of Kentucky, [and] was a credit to the Confederate service, as well as to the medical officers connected with it."

The hospital often took on the name of the chief surgeon in charge at the time, such as Walker's Division Hospital or Forest's Hospital at

Dunns Falls. *Courtesy of Alexa Crane.*

Lauderdale Springs, but the primary referral was "Lauderdale Springs." Next to the hospital was the death house where wounded and sick soldiers spent their final hours before going to their final resting place in the cemetery on the hill.

After a Federal force destroyed their home on Davis Island, Joseph Davis, brother of Jefferson Davis, and his wife, Eliza, settled at Lauderdale Springs.

In October 1863, Jefferson Davis toured the munitions center and defenses at Selma and Demopolis, Alabama, and proceeded into Mississippi. At Lauderdale Springs Hospital, he discovered that his brother, Joseph, was in deep mourning over the loss of his wife, who had succumbed to typhoid fever. She was buried in the Lauderdale Cemetery, just across the road from the Confederate Cemetery. After the war, her remains would be moved to Davis Island.

During the war, conditions were chaotic, including the mail service. With no manpower to plant crops, many slaves left their owners to scavenge the countryside. Some joined the Union troops. Thieves, foragers and Rebel and Yankee deserters took advantage of the lack of law enforcement.

The *Civil War Chronicle* was the only newspaper having correspondents with North and South armies supplying up-to-the-minute news from battlefield and political fronts. Reported on February 7, 1864, from Jackson, Mississippi, was the following:

> *This city fell today, after minor skirmishing to Federal troops of Gen. William T. Sherman's army. Mississippi's capital city is in flames tonight as Sherman has ordered the torch to all public buildings…While Sherman's 25,000-man army is slashing eastward in its drive another Union force left Colliersville, Tenn., today heading south. It is believed the Union strategy calls for the two columns to unite at Meridian Miss.*

In the frosty dawn of February 14, Union troops marched from Marion Road at Suqualena Creek south to the Meridian Road. The Rebels had attempted to slow the Yankees by felling trees, burning bridges and using sniper bullets. But Yankee troops cleared the debris, climbed over the obstacles and repaired the bridges as they marched through Mississippi.

The *Civil War Chronicle* reported:

> *MERIDIAN, MISS., FEB. 14—It is a Valentine's Day this city will never forget. The Union army of Gen. W.T. Sherman marched into the city this afternoon unopposed by any Southern force. Tonight storehouses, depots, hospitals, arsenal, offices and hotels are going up in flames. More than 10,000 U.S. troops have been ordered to destroy all rail approaches, bridges and trestles leading into the city. Sounds of axes, crowbars and sledges can be heard from all points of the compass as railroad track is torn up and bridges demolished tonight.*
>
> *Sherman is reported in foul humor because he found the city bare of Confederate supplies, railroad cars and locomotives that he had expected.*
>
> *Confederate Gen. Leonidas Polk, who now heads the remnant force opposing Sherman, left the city yesterday with all remaining rolling*

> *stock and supplies. War materials and railroad equipment estimated at $12,000,000 escaped with Polk's tattered force but left the city undefended.*
>
> *Sherman is blaming Polk's escape on Gen. W. Sooy Smith, whose Union cavalry division should have occupied Meridian two days ago, according to the pre-planned Federal time table. No word has been heard from Smith. Sherman remarked tonight between pulls on a cigar, "It's a novel thing in war when infantry has to await the motions of Cavalry."*
>
> *But there are some who are comparing Sherman's infantry with the famed "foot-cavalry" of the late "Stonewall" Jackson. In the past seven days Sherman's 25,000 troops have routed the two Confederate forces attempting to unite and stop them, destroyed large sections of railroad track, wrecked bridges, burned buildings and advanced more than 80 miles.*

One soldier recollected that Meridian was a town "destined to be a thriving and business place. Several large railroad buildings, machine shops, and foundry had been erected, and a large number of dwelling houses were under construction, some of which were nearly finished. Others had just been raised, lumber was piled up in various places for the purpose of building."

At the Federals' disposal were a Confederate armory and arsenal where small arms had been manufactured. Recorded in the journal of Trooper Scott of the Thirty-second Iowa was that "much public and some private property was destroyed. Some abandoned dwellings were plundered. It was said that under the trees some of the soldiers slept soundly on featherbeds in this brief camp near Meridian."

On February 16 at 6:00 a.m., Crocker's Division, the Eleventh Illinois Cavalry and one section of the Fifteenth Ohio Battery departed Meridian, while the Forty-fifth Illinois was to guard the bridge across the Okatibbee. On this day, Sherman began his complete destruction of the railroads at Meridian, ordering men to go throughout the town and destroy everything. Veatch's Division destroyed the six miles of Mobile & Ohio track all the way to Marion and then occupied Marion where they looted and plundered the homes.

On February 17, the burning of Meridian continued, melting frost and ice. The Union brigades of Brigadier General Manning Force and Brigadier General Jasper Maltby, both divisions of Brigadier General Mortimer D. Leggett, broke up the tracks south and west of Meridian, using pine from the trestlework and bridges to build flaming piers. The railroad northeast of Marion was left to Brigadier General James Veatch.

Confederate president Jefferson Davis ordered General Joe Johnston to detach troops to General Polk's aid, saying that "Sherman must be stopped at any cost." But General Polk never took advantage of the scattering of Sherman's men across Mississippi. Instead of attacking, he rested his men.

William Pitt Chambers recorded in his diary from Mobile:

> *The enemy has Meridian…We are told that the Country is devastated where they go—that their trail is marked by the smoldering ruins of burned dwellings—that crops are destroyed, and that everything that ministers to the necessities of life is laid waste by a remorseless foe.*

From Meridian on the eighteenth, Sherman drafted orders for the return march to Vicksburg and stayed in Meridian another day. On this day, Soldier Lucius Barber wrote:

> *When within 20 miles of Meridian, our provision train was left back and a strong guard with it, also the sick, myself among the number. Left to our resources, we did just about as we had a mind to. I went out foraging nearly every day. We always went with a forage train and thus enjoyed the protection of the guard. Seldom came in empty. A porker, some chickens, sweet potatoes, always came within grasp. We drew plenty of hard bread from the provision wagons nearby, charging the same to Uncle Sam, and for shelter and covering, we appropriated the Chaplain's blankets to our use.*

Incidents of Choctaw entertainment were recorded by one soldier: "The Indian boys came into camp with their arrows and long hollow canes, and shot at pieces of meat and crackers which the soldiers put up. It was amusing to us to see them gobble it up and put it in their pockets."

On the morning of February 19, with orders from General Veatch, Howe and the Thirty-second Wisconsin departed Marion and proceeded to Lauderdale Springs to destroy the railroad and depot. They went as far as Lockhart Station and demolished the depot but returned to Marion, sparing Lauderdale Springs.

Charles Smith wrote in his diary:

> *We reached the mill about ten and a half o'clock. There are crossroads and a post office called Battlefield. Doctor Davis a Rebel provost marshal, resided here who was taken prisoner by our advance. The mill and his office were burned...Several Indian families lived close by, who say that their tribe* [the Choctaws] *live five miles above and that there are about 500 of them. About 400 Indians have been in the Rebel army but they became dissatisfied and left it. We got a lot of sweet potatoes from Mr. Davis' garden and the forage teams took all his corn and fodder and most of his hogs. There was a large herd of goats but we did not take them.*

Major General James McPherson reported to Colonel Potts the names of the destitute families desiring to go to Vicksburg: "Such of them as can furnish their own means of transportation will be permitted to accompany the train and those who have not the means but who are worthy, may be taken along in the empty wagons. This will be a matter left largely to your discretion after seeing the people and finding out their circumstances."

The 124th Illinois was assigned to the final demolition and burning. The Ragsdale House was burned, as were other houses, some unoccupied, some not, as described by one soldier in his diary: "Burned every empty building and perhaps some where folks lived."

"Sherman's army left fire and famine in its track," wrote one soldier. "The country was one lurid blaze of fire; burning cotton gins and deserted buildings were seen on every hand. I regret to say it but oft times habitations were burned down over the heads of occupants, but not by order."

According to the *War of the Rebellion: Official Records of the Confederate and Union Armies*, Sherman recorded:

> *We accomplished all I undertook. Our march out and in from Vicksburg was well accomplished; we beat the enemy whenever he opposed or offered resistance. We drove him out of Mississippi, destroyed the only remaining railroads in the state, the only roads by which he could maintain any army in Mississippi threatening to our forces on the main river. We subsisted our army and animals chiefly on his stores, brought away 400 prisoners and full 5,000 Negroes, and 1,000 white refugees, about 3,000 animals (horses,*

mules, oxen), and any quantity of wagons and vehicles…For five days 10,000 men worked hard and with a will in that work of destruction, with axes, crowbars, sledges, clawbars, and with fire and I have no hesitation in pronouncing the work as well done. Meridian with its depots, store-houses, arsenal, hospitals, offices, hotels, and cantonments no longer exists.

On a hill bounded by the present Twenty-fifth and Twenty-sixth Avenue and Fourteenth and Fifteenth Streets was the hospital that treated both Union and Confederate soldiers. The prisoner stockade in Meridian was located at the corner of present-day Fifth Street and Twenty-sixth Avenue. Captain J.H. Trezevant's letter of February 1, 1865, to his commandant said:

We are present confined in a stockade with a lot of Confederate prisoners who are there for most every offense and many of them are bad characters, disposed to steal everything they can lay hands on. Our quarters are heated by fire built in the center which fills the apartment with smoke. The grounds surrounding them are very filthy, the [hole] *having been used as a common sink.*

A report on Lauderdale County from an annual meeting of the Mobile & Ohio stated:

All of our bridges, trestle work, warehouses, and station buildings between Union City, Tennessee, and Okolona, Mississippi, a distance of 84 miles, were destroyed. General Sherman's raid to Meridian destroyed north and south of that place bridges and trestle work on 48 miles, and on 28 miles of that distance all of the warehouses, water stations, and as far as possible destroyed the rails and fastenings. From the full supply of rolling stock of the finest quality, we were reduced to one-fourth of what was necessary, and that was in bad condition.

On April 9, 1865, at Appomattox Court House, Virginia, Confederate general Robert E. Lee met with Union general Ulysses Grant to discuss surrender of the Confederacy. The *Civil War Chronicle* reported:

Grant drafted the following surrender terms:
Rolls of the Confederate army to be made in duplicate.

> *All Confederates to be paroled prisoners.*
> *All materials of war to be turned over to designated U.S. officers, except side-arms, horses, and personal baggage of Confederate officers.*
>
> *Gen. Lee expressed his pleasure with Grant's generous terms, then asked if the terms would permit the enlisted men in his army to retain their own mounts. Grant assured him that the terms, as written would not: but added that he would instruct his parole officers "to let all the men who claim to own a horse or mule take the animals home with them to work their farms."*
>
> *Lee responded that, "This will have the best possible effect upon the men. It will do much toward conciliating our people."*
>
> *Grant introduced the members of his staff to Lee while the terms were being copied. He ordered rations sent to the Confederate soldiers.*
>
> *Following the signing of the surrender terms Gen. Lee again shook hands with Gen. Grant and walked to the porch of the house. As he mounted his horse* [Traveller] *and rode toward the Confederate lines every Union officer and soldier in the McLean yard snapped to attention and saluted the grey commander.*
>
> *For the South—and the Confederacy—the war is lost. It is expected that the remaining Rebel armies in the field will follow Lee's surrender. For both the South and the North the war is finished.*

The *Civil War Chronicle*, in an article entitled "No Celebrating," reported from Appomattox regarding the two generals' second meeting on April 10:

> *As Gen. Lee left the surrender ceremony today, Federal army bands began playing and Union cannons began to boom in celebration. Gen. Grant ordered the celebrating stopped immediately. "We do not want to exult over their downfall," he told his staff.*

By April 10, 1865, on the Road to Appomattox, the end was near. The *Civil War Chronicle* noted that from April 10 to 12, "Union and Confederate parole officers meet. 28,000 tattered Confederate veterans march in the rain to Appomattox Court House and stack arms between long lines of Union troops."

RECONSTRUCTION AND THE CLOSE OF A CENTURY

Soldiers returned home to shocking conditions, with farms having gone to waste, fields overrun with weeds and growth, buildings and fences demolished and friends and families near starvation. The number of women widowed during the Civil War, according to government estimates, was approximately 200,000, and the number of children who lost one or both of their parents was 400,000; 10,000 of these orphans were in East Mississippi alone, according to Reverend Dr. T.C. Teasdale, as published in the March 2, 1866 issue of the *New York Times*.

The Mississippi Baptist Convention, during a postwar session, appointed a board of trustees that would aid in finding and funding facilities to care for the orphans of East Mississippi. The facility and property obtained for this orphanage was the former resort hotel and Confederate hospital at Lauderdale Springs.

The children's home opened in 1866. A former professor of Mississippi College in Clinton, Mississippi, Simeon Sebastian Granberry, was chosen as the home's first superintendent. The first physician, Dr. Sidney Kennedy, was from Lauderdale Station. In only a few months, the number of orphans rose from fifty to two hundred. A problem with the title of land surfaced, and the facility was surrendered to the heirs of the original Lauderdale Springs property. However, the Quakers donated their facility nearby to the orphanage, and it operated there until 1878.

Mississippi had eight railroads, with a total of 872.3 miles in operation: the tiny Grand Gulf and Port Gibson (a cotton railroad); the West Feliciana (a cotton road); the Southern, which ran from Vicksburg toward the Mobile & Ohio line at Meridian; the Mobile & Ohio, running the entire length of the eastern part of the state; the Mississippi & Tennessee, being completed between Memphis and Grenada; the New Orleans, Jackson & Great North, which was heading toward Aberdeen; the Mississippi Central running from Canton to Holly Springs; and the Memphis & Charleston, which cut across the Tennessee border counties.

Mississippi was readmitted to the Union on February 23, 1870. Property that had belonged to Mississippi's east central planters was confiscated for back taxes and divided among the tenants. Most original owners never regained their property. Extreme poverty during Reconstruction caused further vulnerability in the South.

The Southern Homestead Act, passed on July 21, 1866, put for sale 46 million acres of public land in Alabama, Arkansas, Florida, Louisiana and Mississippi. This land was divided into 160-acre plots. The first beneficiaries of this land were destitute freedmen needing shelter, sustenance and a way to live off the land they had labored on for years. This law, however, was repealed in June 1876, making the land available at cheap prices to land speculators, most from outside the South.

In 1870, after much dispute and due to Meridian's consistent growth and vigorous railroad activity, Meridian won out against Marion as the new county seat. The population of Lauderdale County at this time, according to Henry J. Woods of the Works Progress Administration (WPA), was 13,462, consisting of 7,051 whites and 6,411 blacks.

That same year, Weidmann's Restaurant opened its doors. In 1868, in Mobile, Alabama, Felix Weidmann had disembarked the boat where he had served as chef and stepped onto American soil. In 1869, he and his wife, Clara, settled in Meridian, where their day-to-day activities consisted of selling fruits and vegetables and hot cups of coffee in the growing industrial town. Their son, Phillip, carried the family tradition into a renowned restaurant business that lasted for over one hundred years.

Remnants of the war, both emotionally and economically, caused an unsettling—like shifting soil beneath an already shaky foundation. The Riot of 1871 has been referred to as "the bloodiest day Meridian ever saw." The Ku Klux Klan and many whites resented blacks for holding political positions and carpetbaggers and Northern strangers, such as Meridian mayor William Sturgis from Connecticut, for controlling the city.

When Joseph Williams, a black legislator on the county's board of supervisors, was killed outside his house, black legislators Warren Tyler and William Clopton called a protest rally. A fire originating at the store owned by the mayor's brother destroyed much of downtown Meridian. Rumors spread that blacks were planning to burn the rest of the city. A mob formed, and Tyler, Clopton and J. Aaron Moore were charged for inciting a riot. A committee was appointed to remove Mayor Sturgis from office, and two days later, a hearing was held at Con Sheehan Hall. There, Judge E.L. Bramlette and a black policeman were shot. Tyler leapt from the second-floor window. He was pursued and killed by a white crowd. It was reported that Clopton was hurled from an upstairs window and after he struck the ground, one of Clopton's adversaries slit his throat. A mob of armed whites murdered at least thirty blacks. Mayor Sturgis escaped the madness during the night. According to *Hate Crimes*, blacks who escaped the riots fled to the woods of Lauderdale County.

For three days, Klan vigilantes ravaged the town. *Public Women, Public Words: A Documentary History of American Feminism* documented the testimony regarding the Meridian Riot of 1871 given by a black woman named Ellen Parton:

> *I reside in Meridian, have resided here nine years; occupation washing, ironing, and scouring; Wednesday night was the last night they came to my house; by they, I mean bodies or companies of men; they came on Monday, Tuesday and Wednesday; on Monday they said they came to do us no harm; on Tuesday night they said they came for the arms; I told them there was none and they said they would take my word for it; on Wednesday night they came and broke open the wardrobe, and trunks and committed rape on me; there were eight of them in the house. I do not know how many there were outside.*

During Reconstruction, other hardships ensued, but none was more devastating than the Yellow Fever Epidemic of 1878. The *Condensed History of the Great Yellow Fever Epidemic of 1878* reveals that Meridian, then with a population of around three thousand, was so well quarantined that "they thought a rat could not get through without being detected." The first recorded case of yellow fever in Meridian was Lewis Carter, a black man, who carried the mail to and from the trains. He died on September 24. Four days later, a white man, John Etheridge, died. By early October, after twelve more had died, only one drugstore remained opened in the town, and trains no longer stopped at the station.

Sister Mary Vincent of the Sisters of Mercy of Vicksburg had traveled to Meridian with a small group "to bring peace and comfort to the parting soul[s]" of all who died of yellow fever, according to *Nurses on the Frontline: When Disaster Strikes, 1878–2010*. But because Meridian had shotgun quarantine in place on the railroad line, she was unable to complete her trip from Vicksburg. Her party was forced off the train in the small village of Chunky, where the party received warm hospitality before traveling back to Vicksburg.

W.W. George Jr., president of the Meridian Aid Society, requested aid for the town. Doctors, nurses and supplies followed, and many worked to stay the epidemic. The last recorded case of yellow fever in Meridian was on November 11. Recorded cases were 382, with 86 deaths.

Mississippi History Now states that by 1900, 36 percent of Mississippi's white farmers were either tenant farmers or sharecroppers, as compared to 85 percent of Mississippi's black farmers, who didn't own the land they farmed.

Pioneer Manufacturing Cotton Mill, established in 1863, had been burned by Sherman's troops but rebuilt in 1867. The Meridian Cotton Exchange and Board of Trade was formed in 1873. Cotton gins, fertilizer factories and warehousing facilities followed, and by 1880, Meridian was a major center for the packing and distribution of cotton and soon to be the largest city in Mississippi.

One-third of the land in the South came under the control of speculators, who profited from harvesting timber. Northern investors stimulated the rise and expansion of the rail center in Meridian and Lauderdale County into the golden era but caused even more subservience to northern industry. After 1877, industry in the South involved mostly shipping raw materials to northern factories by rail, where finished goods yielded higher profits than in southern industry. Industrial growth in the South, therefore, was minimal, and the unregulated techniques of timber harvesting would reap drastic consequences.

Meridian became the state's largest yellow pine and hardwood market. Timber magnates such as Melville R. Grant, born in New York and of

Crescent Turnaround. *Courtesy of the* Meridian Star.

German parentage, and companies such as Meridian Lumber Company became large lumber producers in the South. Meridian Lumber Company also manufactured other products from timber, such as blinds, doors and sashes.

In 1880, Alabamian W.H. Hardy, who had arrived in Meridian in 1872, began his railroad funding efforts for a new railroad line between Meridian and New Orleans, an idea he'd shelved for seven years due to the financial crash of 1873. On one of his survey trips during this project, Hardy stopped for lunch and marked his map where he thought a city ought to be. This city became Hattiesburg, Mississippi, named after Hardy's wife, Hattie, who was instrumental in the founding of Meridian's literary society, the Fortnightly Club, along with Laura Fewell.

Between 1870 and 1890, Lauderdale County was one of the state's most populous counties. The 1884 city directory stated, "Twelve passenger trains and over twenty freight trains arrive at and leave Meridian daily." During the 1880s, the city added electricity, running water, a sewage system, sidewalks and paved streets.

The efforts of Dr. William S. Langley, assisted by Dorothea Lynde Dix, in the treatment of the indigent insane had led to the building of the Mississippi State Lunatic Asylum in 1855 and a second state hospital, the East Mississippi State Lunatic Asylum, located near the Highlands in Lauderdale County, which opened in January 1885. Black patients were admitted to this location from 1885 to 1891 but thereafter were admitted to Mississippi State Lunatic Asylum in Hinds County, where the University of Mississippi Medical Center now stands.

The Meridian Cotton Exchange and Board of Trade was the predecessor of the chamber of commerce. Dozens of manufacturers, packers, compressors, dealers and buyers flocked to Meridian, and by 1883, approximately fifty firms engaged in cotton storage here. In only a few years, more than five thousand workers would be employed in the shops.

Since 1848, peddlers had been paying annual fees to the county where they traded. In Marion, those on foot paid around $100, and those selling from vehicles paid as high as $200. Licenses had been issued to Moses Rosenbaum; Lipman [*sic*] Levy; Aaron, Leopold and Moses Lowenstein; Samuel Loeb; and Isaac Mayer. The influx of Jewish immigrants from Eastern Europe during the late nineteenth century and the later economic success of the Meridian Jewish population allowed for two synagogues in the city. Beth Israel, formed in 1868, embraced Reform Judaism and in 1874 joined the Union of American Hebrew Congregations. A more traditional worship style was held at the Orthodox synagogue, Ohel Jacob.

The Jews in Early Mississippi states that the European House was probably the first hotel in Meridian. In 1879, Charles Wessolowsky wrote:

> *In the morning we departed for Meridian, Miss., where we landed in due time and were greeted by the shout of hotel drummers, soliciting customers for their respective hotels. Being an entire stranger in the city and not knowing what hotel to make our headquarters, we followed one who brought us to the European House, F. Weitman, Proprietor, and indeed, we were pleased with our accidental solicitor.*

In 1872, Mark and Hannah Winner arrived in Meridian and started Winner and Klein Co., forerunner to the Winner and Klein department store located at Twenty-second Avenue and Fourth Street. In the late 1860s, Abraham Threefoot, having changed his original name from "Dreyfus" to "Threefoot," began his establishment with sons H. Marshall, Kutcher and

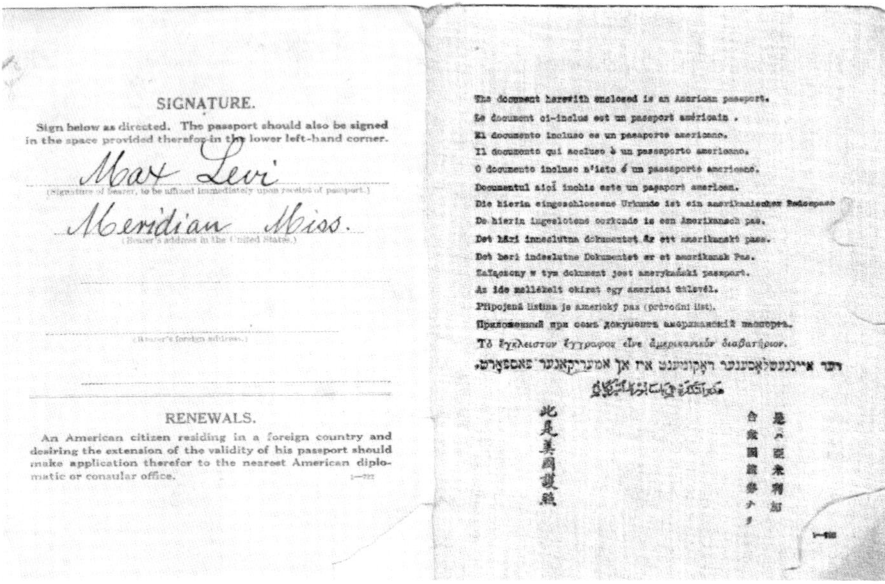

SIGNATURE.

Sign below as directed. The passport should also be signed in the space provided therefor in the lower left-hand corner.

Max Levi

Meridian Miss.

(Bearer's address in the United States.)

(Bearer's foreign address.)

RENEWALS.

An American citizen residing in a foreign country and desiring the extension of the validity of his passport should make application therefor to the nearest American diplomatic or consular office.

The document herewith enclosed is an American passport.
Le document ci-inclus est un passeport américain.
El documento incluso es un pasaporte americano.
Il documento qui accluso è un passaporto americano.
O documento incluso n'isto é um passaporte americano.
Documentul aici inchis este un pasaport american.
Die hierin eingeschlossene Urkunde ist ein amerikanischer Reisepass
De hierin ingesloten oorkonde is een Amerikaansch pas.
Det häri inneslutna dokumentet är ett amerikanskt pass.
Det heri indesluttede Dokument er et amerikansk Pas.
Załączony w tym dokument jest amerykański paszport.
Az ide mellékelt okirat egy amerikai útlevél.
Připojená listina je americký pas (průvodní list).

Moax Levi Passport. *Courtesy of Lauderdale County Department of Archives and History.*

Lewis. The Threefoot name became synonymous with Meridian's wholesaler and retailer of groceries, makers of leather goods and buyers of cotton.

German-born immigrant Israel A. Marks had moved from New York to New Orleans, where he worked as a dry goods peddler. In 1870, he opened a wholesale dry goods business in Meridian, advertising "Choice Family Groceries, dry goods, boots, shoes, and plantation supplies." In the 1880s, Marks consolidated with Lichtenstein and Company, forming Marks-Lichtenstein, which was located at Sowashee Station on Front Street. Lichtenstein left in 1887, according to *Jews in Early Mississippi*, so Marks and his three half brothers, Sam, Levi and Marks Rothenberg, started a new company: Marks, Rothenberg & Company. Their five-story location opened on the block of Fifth Street and Twenty-second Avenue in 1899. The twenty-five- by forty-foot archways into the building allowed a lady's carriage to enter and her to dismount at the open courtyard without getting wet or enduring the blinding heat of the afternoon sun. Preplanning for the growth of the railroad town and the future need for a larger downtown hotel, the building's many windows would allow for future room partitions if it converted from a grocery business to a hotel.

In the 1870s, Boosen, Prussia immigrant Joseph Baum established a large wholesale and retail dry goods store that also dealt in cotton from local farmers. Joseph Baum & Son was located on what was called the "Baum Block." This block extended from Second to Third Street on Twenty-fifth Avenue. A.J. Lyon and Company occupied the Baum Block in 1892. Lyon and his brothers-in-law, Ike and Mike Rosenbaum, were known as east Mississippi's number one wholesale grocers and retained that title for fifty years.

George Wilberforce Soulé moved his Morton and Shubuta operations to Meridian in 1879. He founded Southern Standard Cotton Press Company and the Progress Manufacturing Company, which he sold in the late 1800s. In 1893, he incorporated Soulé Steam Feed Works, which was located at the

Robert Loeb, Nanny and Alex Loeb. *Courtesy of Lauderdale County Department of Archives and History.*

corner of Fifteenth Avenue and Fifth Street. Soulé bought the old Meridian Candy Factory that had been damaged by fire. He repaired the building and relocated Soulé there, adding another building in 1907. Soulé became the highest-paid employer in Meridian. During the timber boom years, the patented Soulé Rotary Steam Engine was used worldwide. Over his lifetime, Soulé patented over forty items.

Alex Loeb had married Mollie Threefoot and moved to Meridian, where he opened his fine men's clothing store in 1887. Known for his fashionable attire, white mustache and a dangling cigar between his lips, Loeb heartily welcomed customers into his store.

Meyer Brothers was a wholesale grocery headed by the sons of Jacob and Henrietta Meyer. The family also had a livery stable and built the Lamar Hotel.

Rabbi Judah Wechsler, Beth Israel's spiritual leader, was a strong advocate of African American education. He led the movement to provide public school facilities for blacks during racial segregation. In 1888, Wechsler campaigned for a bond issue to construct the first brick public school building for African Americans. With the bond's passing, a marble plaque in the new school's corridor read:

> *Wechsler School—This original building was erected in 1888 being the first brick public school building in Mississippi for Negro children and was paid for from the proceeds of a bond issue voted by the white citizens of Meridian. It was named for Rabbi Wechsler on request of the Negroes of Meridian because he led the movement to provide public school facilities for their children.*

In Lauderdale County, Frank Berry, a skilled black man in bricklaying, helped build the Meridian City Hall, the courthouse, the old city and county jails and many other Meridian buildings. Berry was working on the three-story Citizens Bank Building when the scaffolds collapsed. His right leg was permanently crippled from the fall. An injury that could have also crippled Berry's survival as an African American in a segregated South propelled him into great success as a businessman. Berry realized the need for a full-service funeral home for his community. In 1882, he became the first licensed black embalmer and established the first black funeral home in downtown Meridian. In March 1905, Henry Strayhorn Sr. and Frank Berry, both prominent Meridian bricklayers, started Strayhorn & Berry Funeral Home. A blacksmith, George Gardner, purchased one-third ownership, and the name was changed to Strayhorn, Berry and Gardner. When Strayhorn Jr. decided to go into business for himself, the funeral home was chartered under Berry and Gardner.

The Queen City had suffered tremendously from early fires like the Great Fire of 1867 that destroyed a block, including homes along Lee Street (the current Twenty-sixth Avenue south of Seventh Street), and the fires from the Meridian Riot of 1871. Bucket brigades were rarely successful, but no organized fire department existed in Meridian's first twenty-two years. In 1872, a fire district was designated, taking in the area from Hale Street (Twenty-second Avenue), along the tracks to Washington (Twenty-seventh Avenue), to High Street (Sixth Street), to Johnson (Twenty-fifth Avenue), down to Sidney (Fifth Street), up to Lauderdale (Twentieth Avenue) and down to the railroad tracks to the beginning. Here no wooden structures could be erected. Still, fires broke out in 1873 at the Meridian Cotton Mill,

Early firemen of Meridian. *Courtesy of the* Meridian Star.

in 1882 at the city's first cotton compress built by John Ball and in January 1883 at the original First Presbyterian Church, the latter damaging most of the city block.

By 1886, the Mechanic Steam Fire Company Number One protected the central city district; the Finch Steam Fire Company Number Three protected the West End; and the Gem Steam Fire Company Number Five protected the East End. The Excelsior Number Four Hose Truck Company and the Phoenix Hose Truck and Hand Engine Company were next. Meridian began a hook and ladder company, and by 1894, the city fire department consisted of four volunteer companies and one paid company.

Granted a charter on March 6, 1888, Citizens National Bank was first located on Fourth Street between Twenty-second and Twenty-third Avenues. It opened on May 7, 1888, with an authorized capital of $50,000 that had been raised by farmers and businessmen. There were two employees, Walter Brown and Paul Brown. The bank had no safe, so money was put into a tin box at the end of the day. The bank's first loan was for $10, and the collateral

Citizens Bank. *Courtesy of Citizens National Bank.*

for the loan was a gold watch. The loan was never repaid, and the watch was sold for $10. The name of the bank was changed to the Citizens Bank under President W.A. Brown. Founders were W.A. Brown, J.S. Solomon, W.W. George, Thomas H. Woods, C.W. Robinson, Jesse Bounds Jr. and George W. Meyer.

Meridian National Bank would be established in 1902 and the Merchants and Farmers Bank, later known as Deposit Guaranty, in 1906.

The Marks Rothenberg Company, Swedish immigrant and architect G.M. Torgenson and contractor brick mason Charles M. Rubush signed a contract on June 19, 1889, for the design and building of a "block of Five Storey Buildings and Opera House" with a completion date of November 1, 1889. The contract price was $55,400.

Opening on December 17, 1890, the Grand Opera House seated approximately eleven hundred people. To earn the label "Grand," the stage required at least a thirty-foot-wide proscenium and a fly space for scenery that rose above the sight line of the audience. Seats had to accommodate more than eight hundred people, and there had to be enough dressing room space to facilitate thirty-plus actors. Also, there had to be a protected ticket booth to ensure the traveling company's percentage of the profit.

The upper balcony, or crow's nest, seated three hundred black patrons on bench seats covered with coarse cloth stuffed with corn shucks and pine needles. The elite black community benefited from a reserved section in the

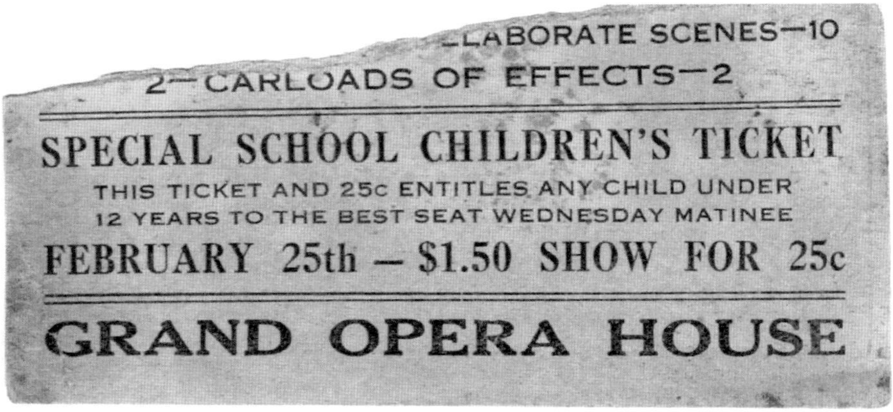

Youth Show, Grand Opera House. *Courtesy of Lauderdale County Department of Archives and History.*

"May I have this dance?" Dance card, front. *Courtesy of Lauderdale County Department of Archives and History.*

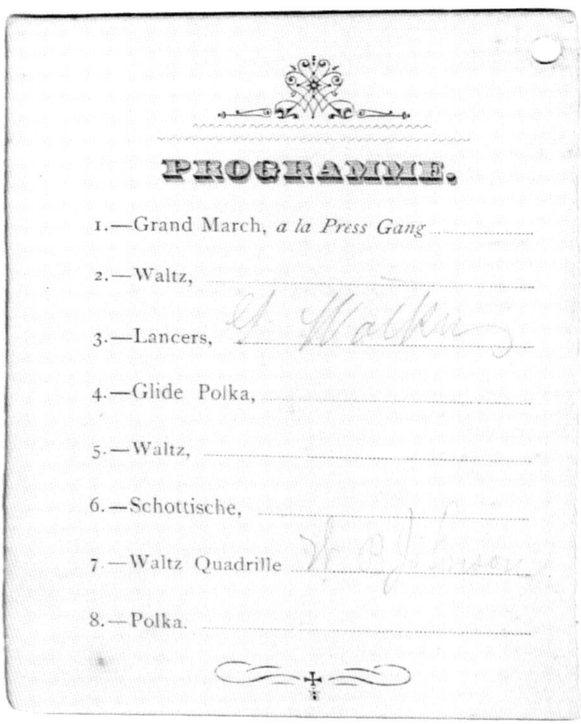

PROGRAMME.

1.—Grand March, *a la Press Gang*

2.—Waltz,

3.—Lancers,

4.—Glide Polka,

5.—Waltz,

6.—Schottische,

7.—Waltz Quadrille

8.—Polka.

Dance card, inside. *Courtesy of Lauderdale County Department of Archives and History.*

front part of the gallery. White attendees enjoyed plush red upholstered seats with racks beneath them to hold a gentleman's hat. They could choose from the "parquet," an auditorium of five hundred seats, or the "dress circle," a balcony that served about three hundred patrons. Shows were booked in the straight line from New York to New Orleans. During intermission, tea and cakes were served to patrons who had made advance orders. Walls and arched ceiling were covered in silver-mounted paper, which reflected the brilliant light from the Sunburner gas chandelier, the gas-lit battens above the stage and the footlights. The eight dressing rooms off the back of the stage included the star's room, which had a coal fireplace.

By the turn of the century, Lauderdale County had fully evolved from a frontier town to a successful railroad city and entertainment hub of the South.

THE TWENTIETH CENTURY

H.M. Threefoot had built the Lauderdale Cotton Mills on the outskirts of Meridian. The mills manufactured prints and colored fabrics and employed 250 to 300 workers, mostly farmers who had faced bad crops due to the boll weevil. These workers settled into the mill communities such as Georgetown and Tuxedo Park. Most had six to ten children and worked ten-hour days. There was no school close enough to the mills for their children to attend. Therefore, many teenagers worked in the mills alongside their fathers.

U.S. statistics in 1900 show that there were 16,855,000 students enrolled in elementary and secondary schools and 238,000 in higher education. However, school attendance would not be mandatory in Mississippi until 1918. To the *Triumphant Democracy*, philanthropist Andrew Carnegie said, "Just see, wherever we peer into the first tiny springs of the national life, how this true panacea for all the ills of the body politic bubbles forth—education, education, education." Carnegie would go on to help fund thousands of libraries all over the world.

I. Marks approached Andrew Carnegie about a library for Meridian, and it became the fifth southern community to receive Carnegie funding: $30,000 for the white library and $8,000 for the African American branch. Both libraries opened in 1913. The first library board consisted of President I. Marks, B.F. Hyde, J.E. Bolton, Ernest Wadsworth and W.E. Jones. The First Negro Advisory Board and search committee for a librarian consisted

Carnegie Library. *Author's collection.*

Meridian Light and Railway. *Courtesy of the* Meridian Star.

of Professor Shaw (principal of Haven Institute), Professor Triplett, Dr. Howard, Jeff Wilson, Frank Berry, Henry Strayhorn, John Harris and other African American community leaders.

According to the 1908–09 City Directory (Vol. 8, *Maloney's 1908–09 Meridian, Miss.*), the population of the "City of Suburbs" was 38,808. Suburbs included College Heights, Asylum Heights, Marion, Poplar

Springs and Bonita. The recorded population outside Meridian was approximately 5,500.

In 1904, S.H. Floyd purchased the J.C. Lloyd residence located on land originally belonging to early settler Richard McLemore, which he deeded in 1859 to his daughter Juriah. She and her husband, W.H. Jackson, built a small residence on the property, according to W.G. Croom's 1882 history. In 1863, the residence was used by General Joseph E. Johnson as headquarters for the Department of Mississippi and East Louisiana during the Civil War. This dwelling is known to be one of the few structures in Meridian spared by Sherman. Floyd extravagantly remodeled this home in the Academic Revival style, and today this structure is Merrehope, an acronym derived from the words "Meridian Restorations" and "hope."

Jewish businesses in Meridian included Levy & Tannebaum Confectionary, Lowenstein & Brothers Grocery, Eagle Cotton Oil Company, Strauss & Lerner Jewelry Store, Metzger & Kahn wholesale and retail grocers and many others.

Major businesses also listed in the directory were:

Bostick Lumber & Manufacturing Co., yellow pine lumber, sash, doors, blinds; T.J. Bostick, president

Union Bank and Trust, E.B. McRaven, president; O.L. McKay, vice-president; J.A. Gibson, cashier; R.C. Weems, assistant cashier; Directors George S. Weems, T.L. Wainwright, J.P. Wetherbee, C. Rosenbaum, O.L. McKay, S.A. Neville, E.B. McRaven, A.J. Lyon, A.H. George, J.A. Gibson, W. Meeds, Sam Meyer, J.F. Miazza, A.C. Hunter, J.R. Dowdle, Dr. T.A. Barber, C.L. Gray, R.C. Weems, S. Lowi, F.J. Burke, F.E. Richardson, E.F. Ballard and T.C. Lyle

Winner, Klein & Co., "Meridian's New Daylight Store," 406–10 Twenty-second Avenue; grocery department, 2112–14 Fourth Street

Mississippi Cotton Oil Company, A Street, corner of Twenty-second Avenue

Meyer & Schamber Jewelry, 2224 Fourth Street, corner of Twenty-third Avenue

Dr. S.F. Riley, Suite 46, Rosenbaum Building, phone 848

Gus A. Rush, dentist, Miazza Woods Building, 1111 Twenty-fourth Avenue

Alex Loeb, Exclusive Retail Clothier, 814 Twenty-fourth Avenue

Gressett Music House, 2302–22 Second Street

Meridian Coca Cola Bottling, 2714 Fifth Street, phone 497

Heiss & Sons Book Store, 2210 Fifth Street, phone 130

Meridian Light & Railway Company

Meridian Male College, M.A. Beeson, College Heights; Miss Mary Wilson, secretary; phone 357

Meridian Star Publishing Co., C.P. Dement, president; J. W. Dement, secretary-treasurer; 2109–11 Fourth Street

Southern Standard Cotton Press Co., C.J. Hyde, proprietor

Grand Avenue Hotel, Leo Lutz, proprietor; H.E. Mann, manager; American rate, $2.00, $2.50, $3.00; European rate, $0.75, $1.00, $1.50

New Kimbrell Hotel, European Plan, Kimbrell & Culpepper, proprietors; Fourth Street and Twenty-second Avenue, $0.50 per day and up

Harness and Saddlery: Bonita Bargain Co., Bonita Gurley; A.W. Sadlry, 2210–14 Second Street; Meyer Bros., 2101–07 Fifth Street; Threefoot Bros & Co., 701–11 Twenty-second Avenue, 812–14 Twenty-third Avenue; Winner Klein & Co., 2112–14 Fourth Street

Hay Presses: Charles J. Hyde, 2109 Fourth Street, phone 234

Horseshoers: R.K. Gough, 2008 Fourth Street; T. Pritchett, 2400 Sixth Street

Horses and Mules: Greenwald & Champenois, 408–10 Twenty-first Avenue

Hotels: Elmore Hotel, 202 Nineteenth Avenue; Grand Ave Hotel, 2200–04 Front Street; Heidelberg Inn, 2308–16 Eighth Street; Hotel Meridian, Twenty-second Avenue and Second Street; Hotel Winston, 2308 Fifth Street; Planters Hotel, 600 Twenty-fifth Avenue; Rogers House, 2122 Second Street; Southern Hotel, 500–20 Twenty-third Avenue.

T.A. Gillespie, Ladies Ice Cream Parlor, South Hotel Building, phone 11

Arundel Lithia Water, water of unparalleled purity, springs located near Meridian on NO&NE Railroad

The *Black Business Directory of 1896–1910*, under the section entitled "Meridian Colored Commercialism," stated:

> *More than fifty business establishments in the Black downtown district of Meridian were owned and conducted by colored men. Among these are two drug stores, that for size, selection and character of stock, equipment, attractiveness and conduct are the peers of any in the State; two undertaking establishments of the highest class—having the finest funeral equipages in the city; real estate corporations owning and renting large brick blocks;*

> *tailoring and millinery stores, hotels, cafes and grocery and other stores in largest numbers.*
>
> *These enterprises are owned and conducted by men of the highest character, business capacity and integrity—men whose credit, standing and obligations are never questioned by white or colored.*

Black businesses during this era were: Howard's Drug Store on Fifth Street and Twenty-fifth Avenue; J.W. Smith Family Groceries and Country Product on the corner of Eleventh Street and Thirty-fourth Avenue; S.A. Rivers, the Reliable Undertaker, 2511 Fifth Street; Allen's Transfer at 504½ Twenty-fifth Avenue; Hotel Winston and Café at 2308 Fifth Street; the American Benefit Association, the only association operated by colored men in the state; the Acme Café at Fifth Street between Twenty-fourth and Twenty-fifth Avenues; Hardy Pierson, drayman, whose grocery store was on the corner of Eleventh Street and Thirty-second Avenue; Sam Water at Seventeenth Street and Thirty-first Avenue; J.W. Foster Grocers and Provisions on Thirty-seventh and Sixth Street; Harry Frazier on Thirty-first Avenue between Seventh and Eighth Streets; F. Edwards, grocer, at Sixteenth Avenue and Twenty-second Street; L.A. Coleman & Co. Restaurant and Refreshments on Thirty-second and Thirteenth Street; Mrs. Lulu Carroll on the corner of Sixteenth and Thirty-first Avenue; Mrs. Florence Burwell at 3200 Sixteenth Street; A.C. Clark, 2116 Fifth Street; John Beal's High Class Pool Parlor at 2411 Fifth Street; the Klondike Skating Rink on Seventeenth Street between Nineteenth and Twentieth Avenues; James & Beal, proprietors; and B.F. Sims, Staple and Fancy Groceries, Cigars, Tobacco, on Thirteenth Street and Thirty-eighth Avenue.

Two new schools were established for the colored children of Meridian: in 1905, East End Elementary School in the Mt. Zion Baptist Church on Tenth Avenue and Eighteenth Street, and in 1902, West End Elementary School located in a two-room building on the west bank of Didley Branch at Seventh Street and Forty-third Avenue. With Professor J.T. Wilson as principal and Miss Emma B. Ivy and Miss Ethel Cole as teachers, East End provided education to fifty Negro students from grades one to eight. Miss Margrette Lacy was the teacher at West End.

The great divide between the black and white races is indicated in the *Illustrated Handbook of Meridian, Mississippi*, issued under the auspices of the

Meridian Board of Trade and Cotton Exchange in 1907. Officers for said exchange during the 1907–08 tenure were S.A. Neville, president; J.A. Gibson, vice-president; B.J. Carter, secretary; and E. Cahn. The directors were Tom Lyle, O.L. McKay, K. Threefoot, E. McMorries, E.S. Bostick, Frank Heiss, C.W. Schamber and M.C. Moore. The handbook was compiled by F.M. Runnels and stated:

> *A splendidly Policed City: Meridian is unquestionably one of the best policed cities in the South…In dealing with the petty crimes, for which a very large proportion of the* negro race [emphasis by author] *is guilty, the department has adopted in large measure the system pursued in many other cities with great success—a dependence more or less on certain informers who may be depended on to locate negroes who are wanted by the chief…There are officers on the force who know the name and personal history of four-fifths of the* negro men and women of Meridian [emphasis by author] *and who know instantly where to locate a man or woman when wanted. As the criminal negro is a predatory individual it is one of the systems of the department to keep a record of the movements of these follows, and when a petty theft is committed and the evidence points to one of these men with police histories, the officers are able to judge with almost certainty to which neighboring city or town he has escaped.*

Elizabeth Cochran and Mrs. J.R. Whittaker realized the need for a school in the Georgetown area for the children of millworkers and helped found the City Mission Board of Meridian in 1904. That location in Mission Hall would be short-lived.

The following was reported in a *New York Times* article on March 3, 1906:

> *Meridian, Miss., March 2.—At 6:30 o'clock this evening a tornado from the south struck Meridian, sweeping directly through the business centre of the town, and during the twenty minutes it spent in passing, destroyed approximately $5,000,000 in property.*
>
> *It took the lives of perhaps thirteen white persons and twenty negroes.*
>
> *At midnight the town is in darkness, the telegraph wires are all down, and the only communication with the outside world is over the long-distance telephone to New Orleans and Mobile…Several fires started in the ruins,*

but the rain and the fire company together succeeded in quelling the flames.

The list of the dead and the wounded is now partially prepared. The dead are MACKEY SLAUGHTER, wife, and daughter; MRS. SINGLETON; CLAUDE WILLIAMS; A.T. McINNIS; A. MOBILE, an Ohio conductor; WILLIAM R. NELSON, City Marshall, and WILLIAM JOHNSTON.

Among the wounded are Capt. CHARLES ELMIRA; W.J. WOODSIDE; T.H. BROWN; ERNEST BENNETT; FRANK WOODRUFF; WILL YARBOROUGH; and A.C. MORRISON.

Several of these are fatally hurt. Nearly all were taken from the debris of the MEYER NEVILLE hardware store.

Two dead men were taken from the JOHNSTON Transfer Company, but they have not been identified. Another is missing. It is reported that in the negro district fully a score of lives were lost and that several houses were burned, the inmates being cremated under the debris.

Among the chief buildings destroyed were:

MEYER NEVILLE Hardware Company's building, on Front Street, seven stories. Loss, building, $100,000, stock, $150,000.

Grand Avenue Hotel, brick, four stories, Front Street and Grand Avenue. Loss, building and furnishings, $50,000.

THOMAS LYLE Wholesale Grocery Company's building, four stories. Loss, building, $35,000, stock $40,000.

ELMIRA Restaurant, two stories. Loss, $10,000.

JOHNSTON Transfer Company, two stories. Loss $10,000.

CULPEPPER Hotel, Front Street and Grand Avenue, opposite Grand Avenue Hotel, three stories. Loss, $15,000.

Young Men's Christian Association Building, two stories. Loss, $15,000.

Freight depot, New Orleans and Northeastern Railroad, partially destroyed, freight damaged. Amount unknown.

Probable damage to electric lighting plant, amount not known.

PEARCE Compress, damages by fire and wind, loss unknown.

...Meridian, which has a population of about 15,000, is the most important manufacturing centre in Mississippi. According to the cenus [sic] *of 1900 its railroad machine shops, cotton mills, cottonseed oil mills, lumber mills and other industries had an output of $2,000,000 a year. It is the centre of a grand and growing region. The Queen and Crescent*

> *route and Southern Railway run through the city. It is about ninety miles east of Jackson.*
>
> *Along the business streets of the city were buildings of five and six stories. Meridian was more like an Eastern city than any other in Mississippi.*

After the tornado, Lyons Brothers Company bought the Baum Block for $25,000. Lyons Brothers operated a large warehouse along the tracks that handled fresh Florida fruit, as well as grain, hay and cotton. Arthur J. Lyons had married Josie Rosenbaum in 1901. A violinist, Mr. Lyons would later help raise money for the war effort by opening his home on the corner of Seventh Street and Twenty-sixth Avenue to music lovers all over the county.

In 1896, John Wesley Beeson had accepted the presidency of East Mississippi Female College, which was owned by the Methodist Episcopal Church South. After the buildings burned in 1903, Beeson purchased land outside Meridian and, with his own money, built the Meridian Women's College. He later combined it with Meridian Male College and changed the name to Meridian College, one of the largest private colleges in the South with one of the largest conservatories of music.

The Grand Lodge of Free and Accepted Masons had "authorized the Trustees of the [Masonic] Home to proceed at once to select a location and

Captain William Beeson and John Wesley Beeson on the Beeson-Baker Farm. *Courtesy of Lauderdale County Department of Archives and History.*

Conservatory of Music. *Courtesy of Lauderdale County Department of Archives and History.*

Masonic Widows and Orphans Home. *Courtesy of Lauderdale County Department of Archives and History.*

erect the Home." On April 15, 1907, the first brick was laid by past grand master (PGM) Oliver L. McKay. Trustees of the Masonic Home Fund in 1907 were John Y. Murry, PGM; William A. Roane, PGM; Thomas B. Franklin, PGM; Thomas U. Sisson, PGM; and Oliver Lee McKay, PGM. On October 15, 1908, sixteen children, ages one through thirteen, and one widow were admitted into

Gallagher Creek. *Author's collection.*

the "Masonic Widows & Orphans Home." The name was changed in 1918 to the "Masonic Home." Later, twenty more acres would be added to the facility.

The parcel northwest of Gallagher's Creek was originally purchased by the Fair and Exposition Corporation, composed partly of I. Marks, the three Rothenberg brothers, W. Rosenbaum and the Threefoot brothers. This corporation dissolved in 1906, and ownership was transferred to a nonprofit organization in which Kutcher Threefoot served as trustee. On July 15, 1908, the property transferred to the City of Meridian on the condition that not less than $12,000 was to be spent by the municipality on the establishment of a public park. On July 22, Mr. John Kamper, lumberman and vice-president of First National Bank, donated the property south of the creek.

As an energized railroad town, Meridian was the perfect environment for "an island of nature." The following statement is by architect Charles Eliot:

> *A crowded population thirsts for the sight of something very different from the public garden, square or ball-field. The railroad and the new electric*

Carousel House. *Author's collection.*

> *street railways which radiate from the Hub carry many thousands every pleasant Sunday through the suburbs to the real county, and hundreds out of these thousands make the journey for the sake of the refreshment which an occasional hour or two spent in the country brings to them.*

Opened in 1909, Highland Park was the premier streetcar pleasure park in the South and the only one in Mississippi, reflecting the importance of Meridian as a major commercial city. Meridian Light & Railway Company provided streetcar transportation to the park and every other section of town except the south side because it couldn't cross the railroad tracks. An example of American Renaissance design, Highland Park's recreational activities included the Dentzel Carousel, Promenade, Dance Pavilion, Bandstand and Amphitheater. Its promenades of concrete paving lighted by hundreds of electric lights were a wonder since most towns had few sidewalks, and only a small fraction had electricity or indoor plumbing.

Mr. Kamper built his house on the crest of the hill overlooking the park and never wanted his view to be blocked. The hillside was traditionally called

Missouri Ridge, the site of a skirmish between Confederate and Missouri troops during Sherman's raid on Meridian in 1864.

In April 1911, two lots were donated to the City Mission Board in Georgetown, and building was begun in the fall of 1911. The Elizabeth Cochran Wesley House, named after John Wesley and Elizabeth Cochran, was opened on February 6, 1912.

Demand for timber was nationwide, and railroads fed that demand. From this timber came the offshoots of turpentine, resin and other wood-processing industries. The railroad provided transportation for all these products. Like timber, cotton also produced a range of subsidiary industries: cottonseed products, yarn, batting and twine.

Timber and cotton were crucial in the rejuvenation of the railroad after the war. By 1912, forty passenger trains passed through Meridian every day, and thirteen lumber companies operated in Lauderdale County. Between 1911 and 1920, the Southern Railroad increased its ton miles—a measure used to calculate freight transport—by over 90 percent. Incorporated in 1911, the Meridian & Memphis (M&M) Railroad also became known as Mud & Misery by those who laid the track through the muddy swamps. In 1929, the M&M merged with the Gulf, Mobile & Northern (GM&N), as did the Mobile & Ohio (M&O).

Lumber and cotton mills sprang up all over Lauderdale County, causing growth and wealth in the smaller communities outside Meridian, such as Suqualena and Pine Springs, where cotton and timber were abundant. Dummy lines, which connected to the main rails, ran from Meehan's Cotton

Union Station. *Courtesy of Lauderdale County Department of Archives and History.*

Long Bell Lumber. *Courtesy of Lauderdale County Department of Archives and History.*

States Lumber Company into the woods around Collinsville and also from Clarke County's Long Bell Lumber Company into the southeastern corner of Lauderdale County, where Whynot and Causeyville also reaped the rewards of the timber boom. The harvest was a special event relished by all, and log rollings were the main attraction.

Other communities benefited from timber, cotton and the rails, such as the predominantly African American community called Wilsondale, named for Professor Thomas Jefferson Wilson, and Chunky Station, where McDonald and Company turpentine distillery had operated, along with several sawmills. T.J. Bostick manufactured the wood byproduct turpentine, which he sold from his Causeyville General Store.

WPA records indicate that Coca Cola Bottling Plant opened in 1904, and its fleet of wagons and trucks served the counties of Lauderdale, Clarke and Kemper and the Alabama counties of Choctaw, Sumter and Greene. The company's daily capacity was twelve hundred bottles. In 1915, the *Evening Star* newspaper, which was founded in 1898 by Charles Dement, changed its name to the *Meridian Star*. In 1919, the oldest saw manufacturing plant south of the Ohio River, J.H. Minor Saw Manufacturing Co., opened in Meridian, attracting business from every state in the Union, as well as Australia, Mexico, Hawaii and Cuba.

Brookshire's Ice Cream Co. was organized in March 1912 and by 1924 had opened its two-story building on the old Brookshire homestead site.

Charles Dement. *Courtesy of Lauderdale County Department of Archives and History.*

WPA field worker Elizabeth Howard stated in her records that few plants in the entire South could compare with Brookshire's equipment, building and manufactured product in purity and excellence. Brookshire's had the capacity to freeze one thousand gallons of ice cream per day. Made from cream and milk from the dairy farms of Mississippi, Brookshire products were classed among the purest in the industry, one of the lowest in bacteria count.

Meridian's first private hospital, Rush Infirmary, was built on February 15, 1915, with one operating room, eighteen beds and one doctor, Dr. J.H. Rush. Dr. Lowry Rush joined in 1921 and Dr. Leslie Rush in 1927. Catherine Hovious, the only registered X-ray technician in Mississippi at that time, remained with Rush for fifty years.

On the corner of present-day Eighth Street and Twenty-fourth Avenue, construction began on the new building for the Hamasa Shriners, which had outgrown its present building. The Grand Ballroom was completed in November 1924. Architect Emile Weil designed the building in the Moorish Revival style with an interior of exceptionally detailed Byzantine motifs. First named the Saenger Theatre because of the contract with Saenger Brothers of New Orleans in 1927, movies and other entertainment were held at the theater. The stage was second in size only to the Roxy Theater in New York. An upgrade to the theater to

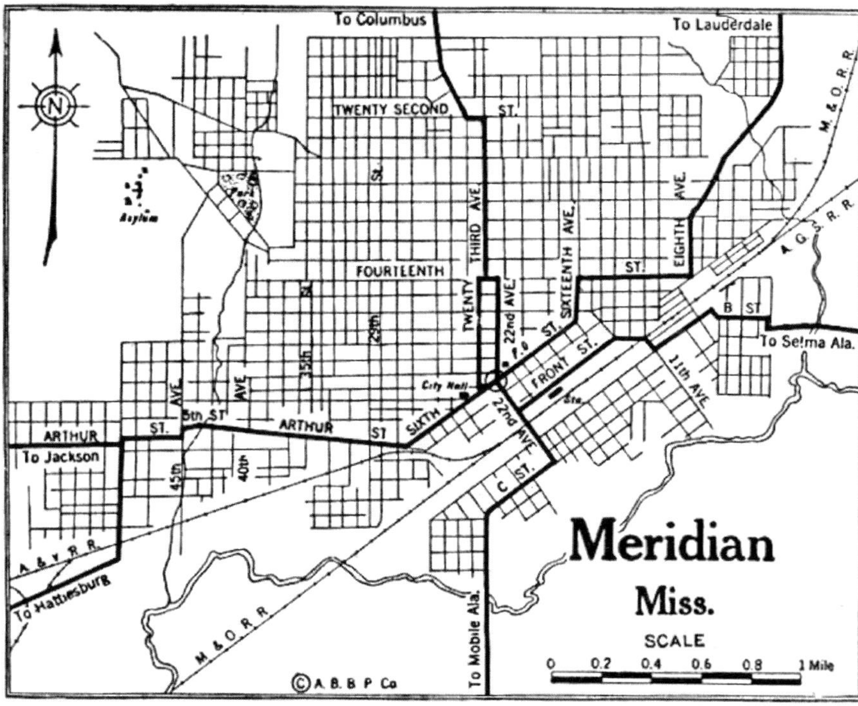

1920 Meridian Map. *Courtesy of Main Street Meridian.*

accompany the silent movies was a Robert Morton Theater Pipe Organ, which is still on-site.

The timber industry created many jobs, but most absentee owners were motivated by the quick profits obtained from clear-cutting. Two-thirds of the timber was depleted in and around Yazoo, Copiah, Rankin, Madison and Hinds Counties. Areas around Meridian within five to eight miles from the railroad were stripped clean. As timber resources were exhausted, timber companies laid off employees, pulled up stakes and headed to the American Northwest. Meridian's rail business slowed to a crawling pace and left little evidence of preexisting mill towns such as Bullards, My and Coonville.

IMPROVING EDUCATION

According to the *1922 Lauderdale County Education Bulletin* report on buildings, teachers and student population, some of the Lauderdale County schools were:

Bay Springs, Miss Hattie Shipp, teacher; A.C. Gould, G.C. Irvy and J.L. Wilson, trustees

Bonita, Virgie Vandevender, Mrs. W.W. Drinkwater and Miss Zella Rawlings, teachers; J.M. McWilliams, P.A. Cook and S.B. Blackwell, trustees

Causeyville Consolidated, L.O. Brown, Miss Reilla M. Still, Miss Mamie Tillman and Mrs. Leila Carr, teachers; H.H. Williams, J.S. Martin and F.C. Hagwood, trustees

Center Hill Consolidated, R.I. Jolly, Miss Maud Harbour, Miss Eunice Wilson, Miss Lola Wilson and Miss Estelle Richardson, teachers; G.V. Richardson, Tom Harbour and Johnnie Snowden, trustees

Collinsville Consolidated School, Schamberville, Mrs. M.W. Ethridge, Miss Lizzie Gill and Miss Clara Davis, teachers; W.L. Walker, E.G. Strange and A.T. Ethridge, trustees

Concord Consolidated School, Meridian, Z.C. Ishee, Miss Esther Lee Ishee and Miss Maude Williams, teachers; B.W. Banes, J.R. Hobgood and Asa Green, trustees

Cook School, Bailey, Mrs. H.E. Sanders and Miss Nora Bounds, teachers; W.C. Bounds, T.N. Gunn and R.A. Brown, trustees

Daleville Line School, Daleville, M.G. Williams and Miss Lala McDonald, teachers; H.T. Mosely, G.W. Cockrell and J.L. Williams, trustees

Dry Creek Consolidated, T.B. Winstead Jr., Miss Reelia McGarrity, Miss Cazzie Simmons and Miss Nora Stephens, teachers; J.M. Taylor, W.Y. Anderson and R.M. Crawford, trustees

Harper School, Russell, J.A. McBride, Miss Valley Rawson and J.E. McInis, teachers; P.H. Lackey, B.O. Harper and B.W. Harper, trustees

Kennedy School, Complete, H.C. Jackson and Miss Williams, teachers; Ross Bounds, Tom Moore and Roy Crampton, trustees

Kewanee-Alamucha Consolidated, Toomsuba, J.O. Giles, Miss Nona Cross, Miss McKheva Nicholson, Miss Lorien Nicholson and Miss Miriam McGee, teachers; Miss Annie Ruth Powell, music teacher; J.A. Boswell, C.H. Ryan and B.J. McDonald, trustees

Lauderdale Consolidated, Lauderdale, W.L. Clayton, Miss Maud Rogers, Miss Florence Walker, Miss Ruby Latimer, Miss Nellie Barnett and Miss Erva Moore, teachers; T.C. Lyle Jr., R.L. Brown and J.D. Rhaly, trustees

Leeville, Duffee, Miss Edna Earl Wood and Miss Birdie Skinner, teachers; W.L. Ethridge, A.T. Brown and H.B. Lee, trustees

Liberty, Kewanee, Miss Mary Lacey, teacher; W.L. Culpepper, J.M. Harding and W.A. Lacey, trustees

Lockhart Consolidated, Mrs. M.L. Pigford and Miss Cecile Butler, teachers; W.S. Pigford, J.F. Null and J.R. King, trustees

Long Creek Consolidated, H.G. Pickard, Miss Pet Smith, Mrs. H.G. Pickard and Miss Della Bethany, teachers; J.W. Smith and J.A. Walker, trustees

Marion School, Marion, J.A. McIntosh, principal; Mrs. C.M. Hobgood, teacher; S.M. Bailey, J.J. Hobgood and J.B. Kinard, trustees

Martin School, Duffee, J.M. Monroe, Miss Rufie Ellis, Miss Arbrett Powell and Miss Angie Monroe, teachers; G.L. Grace, A.G. Townsend and W.F. Clay, trustees

Meehan Consolidated, Meehan Junction, T.E. Nicholson, Mrs. Margie Byrd Moore and Miss Mary Aust, teachers.; T.B. Allen, W.W. Speek and Will Brown, trustees

Oakland Heights, Separate District, E.T. Strange, Mrs. R.O. Caldwell, Miss Marie Sharmon, Mrs. W.C. Sams, Mrs. Geo. Griffin, Miss Elmo Vincent, Mrs. H.C. Jackson, Miss Eleanor Strange and Miss Olivia Buchannan, teachers; Mrs. W.N. Wilder, music and expression

Obadiah Consolidated School, Bailey, E. Horn, Miss Lennis Jenkins and Mrs. R.C. Cunningham, teachers; F.U. Wilson, J.W. Cunningham and R.I. Hooks, trustees

Pine Springs, Bailey, Miss Alma Ratcliff and Mrs. Bessie Calvert, teachers; E.K. Smith, Ed Hooks and W.W. Love, trustees

Ponta Consolidated School, Lockhart, E.J. Jenkins, Mrs. E.M. Jenkins, J.P. Jenkins, Miss Adelaide Gewin and Miss Ethel Cooper, teachers; T.L. Johnson, S.B. Smith and W.L. Clayton, trustees

Poplar Springs Separate District, Meridian, W.P. Still, Miss Ada Holladay, Miss Alberta Jones, Miss Virginia Campbell, Miss Minnie Parker, Miss Maud Mashburn and Mrs. Ruby McDowell, teachers; H.R. Stone, J.J. Houston, M.G. Matheny, G.F. Hand and Percy Johnson, trustees

Rocky Ridge, Duffee, I.M. Thompson, teacher; T.M. Beeman, J.W. Williams and J.M. Hamrick, trustees

Russell School, Russell, Harry F. Murden and Miss Agnes Rawlins, teachers; H.E . Pigford, W.W. Moore and M.L. Simms, trustees.

Sageville School, Meridian, Mrs. Mamie Moore, teacher; P.W. Welbourn, Curtiss Therrell and G.E. Mayerhoff, trustees

Suqualena Consolidated School. *Courtesy of Lauderdale County Department of Archives and History.*

Schamberville School, Schamberville, Mrs. Irma Blanks, teacher; J.A. Scarborough, J.M. Scarborouh and R.C. Barnes, trustees

Suqualena Consolidated School, Meridian, E.C. Morris, Mrs. M.E. Fewell and Miss Venie Dollar, teachers; R.M. Reeves, J.C. Germany and E.B. James, trustees

Toomsuba Consolidated, Toomsuba, Miss Alma Bates, Mrs. J.J. Rigdon and Miss Adna Irby, teachers; G.A.J. Price, W.H. Smith and J.O. Thomas, trustees

Valley School, Meehan, Miss Fannie Blackman and Mrs. Katherine Wilson, teachers; J.A. Ishee, R.J. Johnson and R.W. Houston, trustees

Vimville Consolidated, Vimville, D.A. Fortenberry, Miss Bertha McDade, Miss Lucy Pigot, Miss Ruby Porter and Miss Viola Phillips, teachers; Dr. H.W. Brewster, E.W. Rawson and J.B. Carlisle, trustees

Why Not (listed as two words) Consolidated, Why Not, W.G. Edwards, F.F. Hughes, Miss Maud Edwards, Miss Virgie Dearman and Miss Ruth Tate, teachers; Miss Anna Lee Felton, music; Miss Annie Floyd Robinson, expression; B.A. Nichols, J.W. Gough and J.F. Butler, trustees

Approximately 896 pupils were transported by fifty-seven wagons, and 245 pupils were transported by ten trucks.

The Board of Education for the City of Meridian was K. Threefoot, president; E.S. Bostick; G.C. Kendall; George B. Neville; and J.W. McCorkle Jr. W.C. Williams was superintendent of schools; F.E. Rawls, high school principal; Miss Kate Griffin, junior high principal; Miss Willie Brown, principal of Stevenson School; Miss Ellie Archer, principal of Witherspoon School; Miss Irene Smith, principal of Chalk School; Miss Tilla McDevitt, principal of South Side School; Miss Ursula Majure, principal of Highland School; Miss Virginia Brown, principal of Tuxedo School; and Miss Bulah Thrash, principal of Fewell Survey School.

Not included in the *1922 Lauderdale County Education Bulletin* were the African American schools: Wechsler School, East End, West End, Valley Street and South Side Schools.

The Mississippi-Alabama Business College located in the Suttle Building in Meridian offered programs in business, bookkeeping, stenography and shorthand and secretarial and business management.

More than five hundred boys were enrolled in the four leadings clubs of Lauderdale County—Corn, Pig, Calf and Potato—and some won county and state awards, including trips to the International Live Stock Show in Chicago. Annually, club members made exhibits at the Mississippi-Alabama Fair in Meridian.

The Girl's Home Demonstration Club studied raising poultry, beekeeping, canning, dairying and gardening. A four-year course was given in each subject. After completion, girls were given a certificate worth two units of high school credit. One year, Annie Sue Coats of Oakland Heights Club won the sweepstakes and first honors in the poultry contest at the Mississippi-Alabama Fair and won second place at Jackson State Fair. The motto of the Girl's Home Demonstration Club was "To Make the Best Better." Katherine E. Staley was home demonstration agent for the white Home Demonstration Clubs. Lula Toler was in charge of the home demonstration work for colored people, with thirty-five clubs and 734 members.

THE DEPRESSION

During the boom years, many had invested in risky endeavors and stocks, relying too much on credit. Banks had been careless as well, loaning money to those who couldn't pay it back. Businesses went into mass production when the demand wasn't there. These situations created a domino effect. People couldn't repay loans, so the banks failed. Businesses failed because people couldn't afford their products. Workers were laid off because businesses had no buyers for their products. On October 24, 1929, known as Black Thursday, the stock market crashed, causing many investors to lose everything in one day. This crash marked the beginning of the Great Depression, during which more than five thousand banks would fail and over 12 million Americans would be unemployed. Those who managed to hold their jobs did so at much lower wages. In Lauderdale County, however, many businesses persevered through the grueling times. Determination and fortitude were also evidenced in the new businesses that were established.

McInnis Lumber Company, Inc., was founded by James Earl McInnis in 1922, when Meridian was a hotbed for wholesalers. However, McInnis Lumber not only wholesaled but also financed small pine sawmills by fronting the money so millers could purchase the timber, manufacture the lumber and then sell it back to McInnis, after netting back the initial investment. When the Depression struck, this financing of mills became a great burden, and the company almost closed.

Dr. Franklin Gail Riley. *Courtesy of Lauderdale County Department of Archives and History.*

In 1929, Dr. Jeff Anderson purchased Turner Hospital, renamed it Anderson Infirmary and operated a laboratory, two operating rooms and thirty hospital beds. During the Depression, he mortgaged his home on Twenty-third Avenue to keep the infirmary open.

In October 1929, construction began on Riley Hospital, the first specialty hospital dealing with maternity and pediatric cases in Meridian. Dr. F. Gail Riley, who in 1915 had received his MD degree from the University of Tennessee, became the first physician in Meridian and probably the region to intravenously administer fluid and electrolytes. He was also the first physician to use blood transfusions and the first to use the hemogram as a diagnostic tool. In 1930, Riley Hospital opened as a ten-bed hospital and clinic for children. When the American Board of Pediatrics was formed in 1933, Dr. Riley was certified without examination.

E.F. Young Jr. married Miss Velma E. Beal in 1927, the year he graduated from Haven Teacher's College. In 1930, Velma founded Young's Beauty Salon, the first ethnic beauty salon in Meridian. In 1931, Young bought the barber shop where he worked and from there sold the line of African

Louis Davidson. *Courtesy of Marty Davidson.*

American hair products he manufactured after-hours in his kitchen. Due to the great demand for his products, he received his U.S. Patent trademark in 1933. E.F. Young Manufacturing would become the South's most prominent African American–owned business and would branch out into worldwide distribution.

Russian-born Louis Davidson had arrived at Ellis Island in the early 1900s. He migrated to Meridian, where he started the St. Louis Junk Company and his new southern home. The St. Louis Junk Company became Southern Pipe and Supply Company about 1938.

Some Meridian Jews went into business with non-Jews, such as Harold Meyer and Hunter Webb, founders of Meywebb Hosiery Mills in 1930. Meyer also built the Lamar Hotel, which currently serves as the Raymond P. Davis Courthouse Annex building.

A small wood-frame cottage was donated to Wesley Community House, where after-school activities, food and clothing distribution and other services were provided. A missionary deaconess served the mission. A second floor was added to the cottage, but when the old cotton mill closed, the neighborhood fell into deeper poverty.

The City Directory's statistical review of Meridian, "Center City of the South," stated that the population according to the 1930 census was 31,954. There were thee banks, forty-five hundred telephones in service and eighty churches representing eleven dominations. Chief industries of the city and surrounding territories were manufacturing and agriculture, with the principal manufacturing products being cottonseed products, ladies' and men's hosiery, brooms, mattresses, fertilizers, mixed feeds and grains, woodworking products and brick and cotton mill products. There was one daily and Sunday newspaper and one weekly newspaper. Four hotels housed 460 rooms, and seven railroads rode in and out of the city: New Orleans & Northeastern; Alabama Great Southern; Southern; Mobile & Ohio; Gulf, Mobile & Northern; Mobile & Bigbee; and Illinois Central. The major U.S. highways were 11, 45 and 80, and the state highways were 19 and 39. There were six hospitals, which included five private hospitals and the Lauderdale County Tuberculosis Hospital. East Mississippi State Hospital was located just outside the city limits. There were eighteen public schools and two public libraries, one for whites and one for blacks. Assets of the City of Meridian to prospective homesteaders or businesses included its location, which was 136 miles north of Mobile, 202 miles northeast of New Orleans, 156 miles southwest of Birmingham, 634 miles southwest of Cincinnati and 248 miles southeast of Memphis, Tennessee. State chemists rated the city's water as ideal, pure and healthful, with low rates and the best drinking quality. Also noted were the paved sidewalks and streets of brick and concrete. Meridian's Fire Department was the best manned and best equipped in the South, and its public school system was said to be one of the best in the nation. In the way of entertainment, residents of the city enjoyed Highland Park, country clubs, three theaters providing the best in motion pictures and all forms of sports and athletics. Streetcars had been replaced by buses and private automobiles.

In 1932, a few weeks after Franklin Delano Roosevelt was elected president, he proposed a plan of programs called the New Deal. These programs, most of which became law, were designed to aid the country in a crippling economic crisis. They included the Federal Emergency Relief Administration (FERA), providing funds for local and state relief organizations; the Social Security Act, granting benefits to the elderly and orphaned, as well as people injured in industrial accidents; the Agricultural Adjustment Act (AAA), giving farmers money for the government's request that they bring fewer crops to market; the Works Progress Administration (WPA), providing government funds to construct and hire writers and artists for various projects; the Tennessee Valley Authority (TVA), giving funds to develop the Tennessee River valley; the National Industry Recovery Act (NIRA), creating industry safety regulations and work codes; the Civilian Conservation Corps (CCC), providing environmental improvement jobs to

25 million men; the Farm Security Administration (FSA), lending money to sharecroppers and tenant farmers to assist them in buying land; and the National Labor Relations Board (NLRB), which guaranteed the right of workers to join labor unions and strike.

On January 19, 1932, reformer and progressive conservative Martin S. Conner was inaugurated governor of Mississippi and faced a $13 million deficit. When he left office in 1936, there was a surplus in the state treasury.

According to the Goldring/Woldenberg Institute of Southern Jewish Life, I.A. Rosenbaum, son of Ike, said that when many businesses became strapped for cash during the Great Depression, Ike allowed them merchandise on credit if they had been fair and honest in their dealings. One of these recipient stores was J.D. Clark & Son. When Clark's Presbyterian minister declared that Jews would not go to heaven, Clark stormed out saying, "If Ike Rosenbaum can't go, I don't want to go."

When in the late 1920s the construction of the YMCA almost halted because of lack of funds, the Threefoot family gave a large contribution to

Funeral of the Gypsy Queen Kelly Mitchell at St. Paul Episcopal Church, Meridian. *Courtesy of Lauderdale County Department of Archives and History.*

ensure its completion. However, the costly sixteen-story Threefoot Building built just before the Depression set the business on shaky financial ground, and the Threefoot Building eventually closed.

Many businesses in town closed for Abraham Threefoot's funeral, and the newspaper reported that it was "the largest procession ever seen in Meridian." With that statement, one wonders whether this funeral rivaled the Gypsy Queen Kelly Mitchell's funeral of 1915, which is said to have drawn thousands of Romani people of the Mitchell, Marks, Bimbo and Costello clans into Meridian and to the burial site at Rose Hill Cemetery. The Gypsy Queen died in Coatopa, Alabama, while giving birth to her fourteenth or fifteenth child. Meridian was the closest town that could provide enough ice to preserve her body until gypsy bands across the nation arrived for her funeral.

The pulp and paper industry in the South provided an outlet for parts of the wood that had otherwise been considered worthless. In the 1930s, the price of pulpwood ranged from twenty-five to fifty cents a cord stumpage. But as more and more pulp mills were established and competition for wood increased, the price per cord stumpage increased drastically. Timber men realized they could actually invest in their forests, which in turn helped promote the need for forestry in Mississippi.

President Roosevelt emphasized the importance of establishing national forests. Mississippi senator Pat Harrison, then chairman of the Senate Finance Committee, would be instrumental in designating $50 million for land purchases. Appointed as forest supervisor from August 1933 through June 1940, Ray M. Conarro located, surveyed and purchased lands that designated the original Mississippi national forests. The surveys concentrated on areas belonging to large landowners, such as the Long-Bell Lumber Company, the major landowner of the Quitman unit in Lauderdale, Newton, Clarke and Jasper Counties.

Professor T.J. Harris had transferred to the Wechsler School in 1918. During his tenure there, he added home economics, manual training, stenography, band, athletics, library departments and evening classes. But Professor Harris saw the need for a separate senior high school for Negro students, and he made application through the board of trustees and was approved. In 1937, T.J. Harris Senior High School opened with eighteen classrooms and lunchroom space. A separate structure was built for classes on carpentry, cabinetmaking and radio and, later, auto mechanics, bricklaying, electrical wiring and television. Several hundred World War

II and Korean veterans would receive training in the two-year vocational program. Also through the efforts of T.J. Harris, Meridian became the first town in Mississippi to offer the Boy Scout program for colored youth. Harris also supervised the first Boy Scout camp in Meridian. W.A. Reed Jr. had accepted a position at Wechsler High School as a mathematics teacher. As a coach, Reed took the Wechsler team all the way to the Big "8" Basketball championship win of 1935. Reed transferred from the Wechsler School to become administrative assistant to T.J. Harris.

Lauderdale County may be best known for the "Father of Country Music," Jimmie Charles Rodgers, whose short time as a singer/songwriter transformed American music. Known as the "Singing Brakeman" and "America's Blue Yodeler," the Jimmie Rodgers memorial stands at Highland Park with these words etched deep into the stone:

> *His is the music of America. He sang the songs of the people he loved, of a young nation growing strong. His was an America of glistening rails, thundering boxcars, and rain-swept nights, of lonesome prairies, great mountains and a high blue sky. He sang of the bayous and the cornfields, the wheated plains, of the little towns, the cities, and of the winding rivers of America.*

Born on September 8, 1897, the youngest of three sons, by his thirteenth birthday Jimmie Rodgers had twice left home to entertain in traveling shows. Forced to return home by his father, Rodgers's love for song was not stifled. Jimmie's first job was as a water boy on his father's railroad gang. He later worked as a brakeman on the New Orleans & Northeastern with his oldest brother, Walter, a conductor on the Meridian–New Orleans line.

In 1924, tuberculosis (TB) halted Jimmie's railroad life but allowed him to focus on his music with a new force. Musical history was made in late July 1927, when Jimmie Rodgers and the Tenneva Ramblers were to audition in Bristol, Tennessee, before Ralph Peer, a representative of the Victor Talking Machine Company. Peer agreed to record the group, but when the group couldn't decide how to be billed on the record, Jimmie Rodgers decided to go it alone. Integrated into his songs were the blues, jazz and styles of Tin Pan Alley songs. Tubas, clarinets and ukulele added uniqueness to his music. Rodgers wasn't by any means the first yodeler, but his yodeling songs became a trademark in country music.

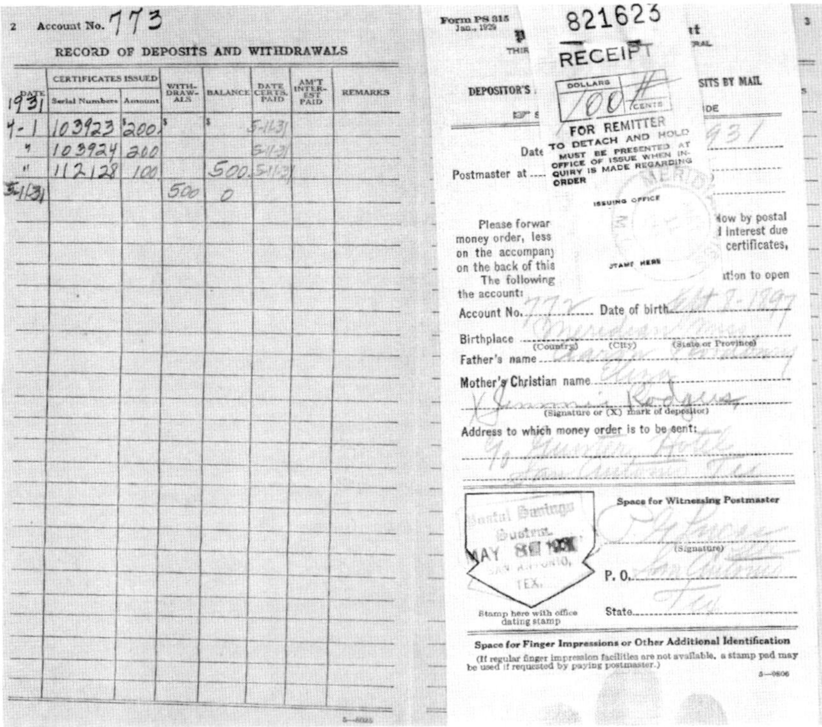

2 Account No. 773

RECORD OF DEPOSITS AND WITHDRAWALS

DATE 1931	CERTIFICATES ISSUED Serial Numbers	Amount	WITH-DRAW-ALS	BALANCE	DATE CERTS. PAID	AM'T INTER-EST PAID	REMARKS
4-1	103923	$200	$	$	5-11-31		
"	103924	200			5-11-31		
"	112128	100		500	5-11-31		
5-11-31			500	0			

Form PS 315 Jan., 1929

821623

RECEIPT

DOLLARS 100 CENTS

FOR REMITTER TO DETACH AND HOLD MUST BE PRESENTED AT OFFICE OF ISSUE WHEN INQUIRY IS MADE REGARDING ORDER

ISSUING OFFICE

STAMP HERE

DEPOSITOR'S ... SITS BY MAIL

Date ... 1931

Postmaster at ...

Please forwar... money order, less ... on the accompan... on the back of this ... The following ... the account: ...ow by postal ... interest due ... certificates, ...tion to open

Account No. 773 Date of birth Sept 8-1897

Birthplace Meridian Miss (Country) (City) (State or Province)

Father's name Aaron Rodgers

Mother's Christian name Eliza

X Jimmie Rodgers (Signature or (X) mark of depositor)

Address to which money order is to be sent: ... Hunter Hotel San Antonio Tex

Postal Savings System MAY ... SAN ANTONIO, TEX.

Stamp here with office dating stamp

Space for Witnessing Postmaster

(Signature)

P. O. San Antonio

State Tex

Space for Finger Impressions or Other Additional Identification

(If regular finger impression facilities are not available, a stamp pad may be used if requested by paying postmaster.)

Inside Jimmie Rodgers Postal Savings Stamp. *Courtesy of Lauderdale County Department of Archives and History.*

According to the *Journal of the American Academy for the Preservation of Old-Time Country Music* article "Jimmie Rodgers" by Charlie Seemann, Rodgers's music inspired a generation of young singers, some becoming legends themselves. Country music historian Bill Malone said in *Country Music U.S.A.*, "In assessing Jimmie Rodgers' influence on American folk music and on a later generation of commercial performers, one can safely use the adjective 'phenomenal.'" Seemann also stated that Jimmie Rodgers directly or indirectly affected over 75 percent of modern country performers.

Known as the "Singing Messenger Boy," Meridianite Bill Bruner performed in the place of Rodgers in 1929 because Rodgers was too sick to perform. Thereafter, Bruner played with Rodgers on several occasions. Bruner received one of Rodgers's early guitars, which Bruner gave to Jimmie Rodgers Snow, son of Hank Snow.

Between 1927 and his death from tuberculosis on May 26, 1933, at the Taft Hotel in New York, Jimmie Rodgers recorded more than one hundred

Man keeping watch over a baby. *Courtesy of Lauderdale County Department of Archives and History.*

songs and sold around 12 million records.

The year of Rodgers's death, over twelve thousand Lauderdale County families were on relief, with eight thousand in Meridian. Vegetables grown in the summer were canned, dried or preserved for winter. Rabbits, or "Hoover hogs," were raised to put meat on the table, and sweet potatoes were stored in soil banks. Store-bought bread and coffee became luxuries, and flour sack clothes became the latest fashion.

The WPA, NYA and CCC put some men back to work setting out trees and building roads and dams for lakes. Two results of the CCC program were Ray Stadium at Meridian High School and Clarkco State Park, located just across the Lauderdale County border in Clarke County. Kudzu was also planted to stop the erosion caused from the over-cutting of timber, but the southeastern climate was simply too perfect for growth, resulting in intrusive vines that could, during summer, climb a foot per day into trees, up power poles, over bushes and across anything else in their way. The vines strangled trees and bushes and kept them from needed sunlight, thus defeating the plant's purpose

Mrs. Elizabeth Howard, a field worker for WPA, wrote that the Philips-Jones Factory opened in Lauderdale County on November 13, 1934, and produced eight hundred dozen shirts with a capacity of one thousand dozen per day. More than five hundred workers manned the four hundred machines. Soule Steam Feed Works included pattern shops, iron and brass foundries, machine shops and assembly floors and manufactured patented steam engines, hoist, lumber stackers and other specialties for the lumber industry. Distributions were focused on Southwest oil regions and lumbering regions of the United States, Canada and other foreign countries. There were ninety industrial plants in Meridian, which encompassed a trade territory of more than one hundred miles in radius. Other enterprises that managed to stay in business during the Depression were Brookshire's Ice Cream Co., White Lumber & Supply (specializing in long-leaf yellow pine lumber, cypress singles, composition roofing, paint, windows, doors, trim and other building materials), Coca Cola, F.A. Hulett, Maywebb Hosiery Mill, Tell Farmer Printers (established about 1895), Liberty Shop (owned by Karl Meyer and William Blum) and J.W. Sanders Cotton No. III off Eighth Avenue and Highway 45, which employed around three hundred men and women.

N.E. Katz, who opened Katz Chemical Laboratory in 1917, hailed from Germany. He was a licensed grain inspector who analyzed cottonseed products, fertilizers, feedstuffs, water and petroleum products. Meridian Brick Company, organized in 1924, operated on twenty-three acres and produced millions of bricks a year. Federal Chemical Company, a manufacturer of commercial fertilizers, was located at Railroad and Forty-ninth Avenues. Emmons Brothers, organized in 1892, produced perfect layer mattresses of fifty pounds of cotton carded by the finest Garnett machinery. There was also Meridian Grain and Elevator, which made the first prepared animal feed in Mississippi. At the death of owner W.S. Harris, it was purchased in 1912 by John H. Harris, J.E. Redus and J.M Wilson. Queen City Broom Company was located at 2320 Second Street and manufactured twelve grades of brooms with the largest machine equipment in the state and one of the largest in the South.

Five miles from Meridian on Dekalb Road, sitting on eighty acres, was Sinclair Floral Company, where thousands of flowers, like verbena, queen's wreath, peonies, calla lilies, poinsettias, chrysanthemums and Dutch irises, grew in open fields and under the semishade of lath shelters. These flowers were shipped to wholesalers throughout the country.

Meridian's struggling airport was managed by brothers and flight instructors Al and Fred Key. They brainstormed an idea to not only bring worldwide publicity to the dying airport but also make aviation history. The idea was to set a flight endurance record—even though they didn't own a plane.

According to Leslie M. Joyner's *James Hamilton Keeton and His Planes*, James Keeton had taken flying lessons and received his license in 1933 from the Key brothers. He purchased a used Curtiss Robin single-engine plane and operated Keeton-Parker Flying Services out of Bates Field in Mobile, Alabama, spending his free time as a stunt airplane performer. He got wind of the Key brothers' plan and wanted in.

The Key brothers borrowed Bill Ward's Curtis Robin high-winged monoplane, which they named Ole Miss, with a 165-horsepower Wright Whirlwind engine, a 150-gallon gas tank and a catwalk. Keeton would use his Curtiss Robin to refuel the Ole Miss and transfer meals to the Key brothers four times a day.

Difficulties during the first flight on June 21, 1934, forced a landing. From that point, two-way radio communication was made possible by Ben Woodruff. Now problems could be communicated to the ground crew, and parts could be air delivered. Radio communication also warned of advance weather conditions, allowing the Key brothers to avoid bad weather areas.

Ole Miss. *Courtesy of Lauderdale County Department of Archives and History.*

Al and Fred Key. *Courtesy of Lauderdale County Department of Archives and History.*

Blind flying instruments were provided by Captain Claire Chennault of the U.S. Army Air Corps, making the Ole Miss the first privately owned plane to use these instruments. Because of strong winds, in-flight refueling was difficult. To remedy this, weights were added to the refueling hose. Ground crew member A.D. Hunter, a machinist at Soule Steam Feed Works, fashioned an automatic shut-off valve for when the hose dislodged from the tank. But the faucet, which required several turnings before releasing the fuel, caused another problem. Keeton used a blowout valve from his family's dry-cleaning business that required one ninety-degree turn to produce a spill-free, air-to-air refueling nozzle. This nozzle became the prototype used by U.S. bombers in World War II. Experimental flights were made to test the refueling equipment. To prepare for a night landing, the locals planned to park their vehicles on the airfield, aiming their headlights toward the landing strip.

The airplanes made it through a near-miss midair collision, a fire on board and 52,320 miles of nonstop flight. In-flight fuel and supplies had been delivered to the Ole Miss 438 times.

After twenty-seven days, totaling 653 hours and thirty-four minutes, the Key brothers landed on July 1, 1935, and still hold the flight endurance record. The Ole Miss is on permanent display in the National Air and Space Museum.

More Lauderdale County history was made in 1936 when Dr. Leslie Rush of Meridian performed the first recorded bone pinning in the country. The "Rush Pin" is still used for fractures. Dr. Leslie Rush would also be instrumental in starting Mississippi's first junior college and hospital nursing school in 1944.

THE '40S AND '50S AND TWO WARS

On September 1, 1939, *Meridian Star* headlines declared, "Fierce Attacks by Germans upon Poland's Capital." Another headline read, "F.D.R. Certain U.S. Will Stay Out of Big War."

On Wednesday, September 27, 1939, an officer from the U.S. Army Inspector General's Office inspected the newly formed 153rd Observation Squadron at Key Field. The next day, the Meridian City Council authorized the leasing of Key Field for twenty years to the federal government, specifically for the 153rd. The sum of $1,965,000 had been allocated for Meridian's civilian airport, which would include three paved runways and one that was graded.

Flintkote of Meridian and DeWeese Lumber Company in Neshoba County were among the first to hire actual foresters. Flintkote purchased cutover land in eastern Mississippi, comprising approximately ninety thousand acres that served as a pulpwood reserve for the Meridian plant. Arthur W. Nelson Jr., who had earned his BS degree in forestry at the University of Idaho and a master's in forestry from the Yale Forest School, was hired by Meridian's Flintkote in 1940 to handle the forestry and timber procurement for a new wood fiber insulation board mill. At the time, the company's properties consisted of mostly abandoned, submarginal land. *Mississippi Forests and Forestry* states that Nelson was impressed with the incredibly fast timber growth, and he said that "if nature was given just half a chance—a little fire protection—saving some seed trees—the forest would start on its way back." From his observations of the "cut out and get out" era, he noted that because lumbermen harvested mostly two- to three-hundred-year-old trees in a neglected forest, they believed it would take too long to wait for another crop to mature to cutting age. The term "old field stand" originated from an abandoned field left over from clear-cutting that had seeded up.

The president of the Flintkote Company, I.J. Harvey, announced on February 13 that his board had approved a $2 million factory to manufacture a line of wood fiber decorative and structural insulation and wallboard products that would be located on Airport Road, otherwise known as U.S. Highway 11 South. The company also announced that anyone who was drafted or volunteered under the new military service act would be reemployed afterward.

During the '40s, favorite shopping places included Marks-Rothenberg and the Cinderella Shop, both located on Fifth Street in downtown Meridian. Starting up in September would be the School of Music on Ninth Street and Twenty-eighth Avenue. Mrs. E.H. Hart and Ethel and Margaret Tarry would teach piano; Mattie Sue Tarry would teach violin; Annye Long would teach voice; and Bessie May Tartt, dramatic art.

Movies were the top entertainment choice, and there were several theaters to choose from like the Saenger, the Alberta on Twenty-third Avenue and the Strand Theater, which also had an organ. Its entrance was on Seventh Street, near the Solider Monument.

On January 6, 1941, Lloyd Royal opened the Royal Theater across from Paragon Book Store. The opening feature was *Spring Parade*, starring Deanna Durbin.

On February 26, as about five hundred watched the Royal screen, a tear gas vial broke in the front of Royal Theater. The audience fled. On February 6, a similar vial had been found in the balcony but was never broken. Two days later, a second vial was crushed. On March 28, when Royal was in Gulfport, a small explosion happened about 8:00 p.m., and officers discovered the remains of a device consisting of a dollar pocket watch, center switch, dry cell batteries and what was left of the bomb. In February 1942, Leo Schwartz was convicted for setting off the time bomb and received a ten-year sentence, which he appealed.

In March 1941, Southern Railway unveiled its new streamlined passenger train, the Southerner, and it arrived in Meridian on March 20, complete with the bar car. At this time, Mississippi was legally dry. In addition to the railroad, the bus lines serving Meridian were Greyhound, Tri-State, Trailways and Gulf Transport Company, a subsidiary of the Gulf, Mobile & Ohio Railroad.

Meridian was described by *Forbes Magazine* as one of America's best cities for business. Weidmann's had advertised that Gene Austin, whose company would appear in *Models and Melodies* under its huge tent theater, had selected Weidmann's as his dining place. An autographed photograph of Austin hung in Weidmann's for many years alongside other celebrity photos. Mr. and Mrs. Duncan Hines, authors of *Adventures in Good Eating*, *Lodging for a Night* and *Adventures in Good Cooking*, included Weidmann's in *Adventures in Good Eating*.

During the dog days of summer, at Highland Park, white children swam in the new swimming pools and played deck tennis, volleyball, croquet, shuffleboard, table tennis and softball. New housing was needed for the city's growing population. Life was safe, productive and happy even though other parts of the world were at war.

On Sunday, December 7, 1941, at approximately 1:40 p.m., the Japanese bombed Pearl Harbor. The telegram to the White House read: "AIR RAID PARK HARBOR—THIS IS NO DRILL." Pearl Harbor's death toll escalated to twenty-four hundred servicemen. Over 347 airplanes were damaged or destroyed, according to *Time-Life*'s *Decade of Triumph*. The headline in the *Meridian Star*'s extra edition that night read, "Japs Declare War on U.S.; Attack Honolulu, Guam."

Decade of Triumph, The '40s states that the marriage rate in the United States after Pearl Harbor soared to a rate of one thousand women marrying servicemen a day. Winston Churchill popularized the two-finger victory salute, and the "V" sign was mass-produced on pins, brooches, drinking glasses, home brochures, fried chicken boxes, playing cards, tote bags and more.

Lauderdale County Schools conducted air raid drills, and large bins were placed on site for scrap paper, metal and rubber. Black and white schools competed to see who could contribute the most usable scrap each month. U.S. Army guards were placed at vital locations in the city, such as railroad, rail and highway bridges.

Cigarettes, soon to be in short supply, were a favorite gift to soldiers. Residents grew vegetables in victory gardens. In 1941, the Meridian Wildcats voted to dispense with their annual banquet to contribute seventy-five dollars to the special war relief that the Red Cross was raising. Wrapping paper, magazines and cardboard boxes were sold and the money used to operate the Red Cross's workrooms. Professor T.J. Harris said, "All citizens are urged to be present and contribute as liberally as possible, manifesting the same spirit of loyalty, devotion, and patriotism to the country that has so nobly characterized the Negro in past wars and crises through which our country has passed."

Dr. DeWitt A. Buckingham signed on as medical director and surgeon-in-chief at the new Colored Clinic located at 2506 Fifth Street. Other physicians were Drs. L.F. Brooks, R.F. Spears and J.C. Macon. The dental staff consisted of Drs. H.W. Wilson, W.B. Block and A.B. Blackwell. Nurses were Louise Tyler, GN, and Bertha Jack Emerson, RN. With desegregation in the white hospitals and clinics, Buckingham's clinic offered twelve beds, fluoroscope and X-ray rooms, an operating room and a laboratory. Plus, there were consultation and reception rooms.

There was a freeze on vehicular tires, which prohibited the use and sale of automobile, truck, bus, motorcycle, farm implement or other types of tires or tubes. There was also the rationing of sugar. Many purchased war

Entertaining the troops. *Courtesy of Lauderdale County Department of Archives and History.*

bonds and stamps to raise money for the war. Taxes were raised, and there were discussions of commandeering private vehicles for military use and the necessity for civilian services.

Meridian at War states that under the direction of the WPA's recreational director of the city, Istalena Pace, the following Meridian women would help provide entertainment for the enlisted men:

Mrs. Bernard O'Neil, church parties
Mamie Carter Crumpton, music
Mrs. L.L. McAllister, parties and games
Bessie Smith, dances
Madams Irving Rothenberg and Sylvan Straus, bridge
Marjorie Woods Austin, dramatics
Mary Bright Williams, magazines, books and other periodicals
Maude Smith, literature

The United Service Organization (USO) was organized to provide entertainment for the American troops. Local organizers first met at the Lamar Hotel. Headquarters would be the office of the Meridian Chamber of Commerce, 204 Lamar Building. J.W. Dement was chairman of the men's division, with co-chairmen L.T. Keeton and Earl McGinnis. Chairwomen were Mrs. Thomas L. Bailey and Mrs. M.R. Adams. Female volunteers included Mrs. F.W. Kahlmus, Mrs. Charles Gillespie, Mrs. Leroy Rush, Mrs. W.B. Lowry, Mrs. Battle Crooks, Mrs. John Weems, Mrs. Leslie Rush, Mrs. R.S. Majure, Mrs. W.W. Dawson, Mrs. B.F. Cameron, Mrs. Tom Breazeale and others. St. Patrick's Catholic Church would also form one of Meridian's USO clubs.

A temporary USO club opened in the Marks-Rothenberg Building. At the Seventh Street USO, regular dances, bridge, bingo, pool and wiener roasts were held. At this time, there was no USO for black soldiers.

U.S. representative Ross Alexander Collins, a Meridian resident and member of the House Armed Services Committee who was instrumental in getting authorization for a new squadron in Meridian, was also instrumental in the major million-dollar improvements of the National Guard unit already at Key Field. In January 1942, after urging unity in the military, Collins said, "An inexperienced listener heard the planes in the airplane detectors and passed this information on to a lieutenant who knew nothing about it. This lieutenant assumed the planes heard were those of this country. There could have been no such assumption if command was unified so that there was a check at all times as to just what U.S. planes were in the air."

One goal of the Southern Leadership Training School was to rival Tuskegee Institute. The Meridian Civilian Defense Council and Professor T.J. Harris sponsored a black town meeting in the city hall's auditorium, where attendees filled out volunteer blanks and were assigned to one of the many groups that would participate in the city's defense work. On August 23, 1941, in the WPA Recreation Hall at Frank Berry Courts, groups like the Harlem Glee Club, the Swellites Bridge, the Cotillion Singers and the Spicy Mixers Whist entertained the black soldiers. Hostesses at the WPA East End Recreation Club Chat and Dance event were Bessie Beale, Rosa Barlow, Fannie Johnson White, W. Mae Terrell, Delia Mason Cole and Mamie Floyd. Slayton Evans began the festivities with the Negro National Anthem and "God Bless America," followed by Tereatha Lewis singing "The Rosary."

Women, in cooperation with the Red Cross Motor Corps program, were attending classes at the National Youth Administration three days a week to learn the parts of an automobile and the proper care and service of emergency vehicles.

The Delta Beta Sigma (DBS) sorority played hostess to various events at the Seventh Street USO. When the legislature threatened to outlaw Greek-letter organizations from the state's public school, sorority member and second national vice-president Regina Thornton appeared before the Mississippi legislature to argue against the proposed action.

Under the direction of WPA recreation leaders and the sponsorship of the WPA, residents of the George Reese Court, the Berry Courts and the Baptist Seminary playground performed together for the white Civic Center on February 17, 1942. The African-American Non-Commissioned Officers Club of Key Field held special events as well, such as the September 18, 1942 dance and banquet. Guests that night at the Soldier Services Center would be the 777th Quartermaster Corps. East End School teacher Ruby Wright sang "Indian Love Call" for the soldiers.

At the recommendation of Dr. H.M. Ivy, who served as Meridian superintendent of schools from 1923 to 1952, Meridian Municipal Junior College became part of the Meridian Public Schools in 1937 and enrolled 132 students into the thirteenth grade. A small vocational program was

Ross Collins Vocational Building. *Courtesy of Ross Collins Vocational Building, Meridian Public Schools.*

Gunner Rescues Pal from Flames

— AIR SUPPORT STATION, England, June 16—S/Sgt. Charlie G. Cook, of Meridian, Miss., was awarded the Soldier's Medal by Col. Wallace W. Millard today, for rescuing Sgt. Harry M. Smith, of Corpus Christi, Tex., from a burning plane on May 15.

Both Cook and Smith were gunners on an observation plane returning from an operation. Just before the plane landed it caught fire, and by the time it stopped rolling, the wings and fuselage were blazing.

Cook climbed out the turret of the ship and was ready to jump. He glanced over his shoulder to make sure Smith was there and saw the other gunner enveloped in smoke and partly overcome, his parachute caught on part of the rigging.

By this time the plane was in danger of exploding. Cook climbed back down into the plane, disregarding the flames and the impending explosion, and freed Smith. After getting him out of the plane, Cook helped carry Sgt. Smith clear of danger. The plane exploded a few minutes later.

Newspaper article on war hero and Meridianite Charlie G. Cook. *Courtesy of Lauderdale County Department of Archives and History.*

added in 1938. With funds from the National Youth Administration, in 1942, Ross Collins Vocational Building was built, offering extensive programs for adults and youth. Over fifteen thousand war production workers were trained in the fields of shipbuilding and aircraft repair. At the close of the war, returning veterans, through the GI Bill, were trained in the areas of cabinetry, welding, automotive and diesel mechanics, sheet metal work, radio and television. Night schools for veterans who couldn't attend day classes grew out of the GI Bill in the 1950s.

War was in the forefront of everyone's lives, but daily business continued in Meridian, as one *Meridian Star* staffer observed: "Money, important money, was in circulation on a big scale." Stores were being remodeled, and hotels were full. On street corners, buses delivered residents to and from destinations. The summer of '42 saw the Vogue on Fifth Street advertising a sale and Brookshire's Drive-In on Eighth Street preparing juicy burgers and scrumptious ice cream dishes. Butler's Shoes and Jimmie's Spaghetti House had just opened on Eighth Street, and at Albright and Wood Drugs, one relished a twenty-cent breakfast of eggs, grits, two bacon strips, toast, jelly and coffee.

On Labor Day 1942, the day the Wallace Brothers Circus came to Meridian, over 220,000 pounds of scrap had been collected, and by September 20, the *Meridian Star* reported that the county had exceeded 1 million pounds.

County home demonstration agent Katherine Staley prompted residents to save all fats, which would be used in making glycerin for explosives. Deliveries could be made to Gilbert's Market at 703 Thirty-fifth Avenue; Giant Food Store on Ninth Street and Twenty-third Avenue; Boutwell's Grocery at 1320 Sixth Street; and City Meat Market at 2308 Fifth Street.

To encourage racial harmony, on October 18, 1942, an interracial meeting held at city hall included Reverend Drs. N. H. Jeltz and E.A. Mays from the black community and Reverend Drs. T.M. Brownless, Alfred Mathes and William L. Compete Sr. from the white community.

Reverend R.L. Young chaired the money drive for the National War Fund and Community Chest. The Negro Civic Association also participated in the drive. President of the association was Dr. L.F. Brooks. Other officers were R.L. Coleman, Esther Butler, B.T. Walker, L.S. Beale, E.F. Young, C.W. Williams, T.J. Harris, S.C. Barlow, J.A. Burns, B.W. Coates, C.O. Inge, N.H. Jeltz, W.A. Reed, M. Oliver, A.L. Fielder, Frank Hodges and F.L. Thames.

Memory Lane consisted of flowering shrubs, evergreens and many native trees from Thirty-ninth Avenue and Twelfth Street to Harris High that had been planted by black students.

A goodwill unity service, again including black and white clergy, was held at First Presbyterian Church on February 13, 1943. Race Relation Sunday was held on Valentine's Day at Central Methodist Church, sponsored by the Lauderdale County Ministerial Association and the Negro Ministers' Alliance.

Donations of much-needed blood could be made at Newberry's five-and-ten, Weidmann's Restaurant, S.H. Kress's five-and-ten and Hunt's Pharmacy.

Above: Hardin's truck. *Courtesy of Phil Hardin Foundation.*

Left: Phil Hardin. *Courtesy of Phil Hardin Foundation.*

On June 29, to aide in the Fifth War Bond drive, hundreds of soldiers marched the streets of Meridian along with bands from Meridian High, Flora and Keyfield. Girl and Boy Scouts, the Red Cross, Smith's and Hardin's Bakeries, city schools, stores and the Flintkote Plant took part as well.

Due to wartime restrictions, Seven-Up, Pepsi Cola, Nehi, Coca-Cola, Dr. Pepper, Double Cola and Hires bottling companies started a recycling program for soda bottles.

On April 12, 1945, the death of President Franklin Delano Roosevelt shocked the world. It would be Vice President Harry Truman who stepped into the presidency and authorized the atomic weapons against Japan.

Just before war's end, a series of lectures by Charles A. Wells called "Religious and Racial Persecution at Home and Abroad" was held at First Baptist Church in Meridian. In these lectures, Wells compared American prejudice to the Nazi horror. By the end of 1945, 140,000 people had been killed in Hiroshima and 80,000 in Nagasaki. The final surrender documents of Japan were signed on September 2, 1945.

Lauderdale County's total casualties of World War II numbered 370. And war wasn't over.

In the early morning of June 25, 1950, the North Korean People's Army, under the command of General Chai Ung Jun, invaded South Korea. That same year, President Truman announced U.S. intervention.

Mid-Century Marines, in the Lauderdale County Department of Archives and History, records a meeting at Key Field Armory on October 13, 1947, that set the groundwork for a local U.S. Marine Corps Organized Reserve, of which the first members were Captain B.W. Matthews, Lietenant J.H. Buckalew, Lieutenant Bobby Culpepper, Lieutenant J.H. Mays, Lieutenant W.R. Cable, Lieutenant J.T. Bonner, Steve Purdy, J.F. Burnett, E.E. Hargon, V.B. Palmer, L.V. Covert, C.M. Prouty, H.L. "Buck" Jones, W.A. Rayner, H.R. Jenkins, B.G. Rawlings, W.E. Switzer, W.C. Warren, T.V. Fuller, H.C. Gustin, W.J. Willoughby, J.L. Hargon, T.G. Glover, H.J. Wyche, C.M. Smith, J. Culpepper, C. Culpepper, C.R. Rein, R.E. Lee, R.P. Craven, J.N. Gordon, Lieutenant J.H. Tays, Staff Sergeant C.W. Roth and Sergeant A.W. Weeks. This unit would be sent to Camp Pendleton.

A *Meridian Star* article stated that "men composing 'C' battery are residents of Meridian, Kewanee, Duffee, Collinsville, Quitman, Stonewall, Enterprise and several other outlying communities."

Hoot Gipson arrived in Korea on June 5, 1951. Gipson was assigned to Mike Battery, the same unit as his hometown friend Jimmy Walker. On June 6, they were placed in the Fourth Battalion. Another friend joined them on gun number one: Leroy Morse.

Charles Young, son of E.F. and Velma Young, served in the U.S. Army during the Korean conflict and was awarded the Bronze Star and other service medals.

Families of those who died in the Korean conflict would receive letters of condolence that read something like this: "The untimely and tragic loss of _________, who met his death on the field of battle in Korea, has shocked us all deeply. Some measure of comfort may be derived from the knowledge that he died in the service of his country and in the defense of a peace-loving people."

In 1953, the ship USS *Menard* safely returned many Meridian marines back to the United States.

ENTERTAINMENT

The '50s

In the 1950s, downtown was still the heart of Meridian, with its main arteries being Sixth, Seventh, Front, A and B Streets, as well as Twenty-second, Twenty-third and Twenty-fourth Avenues. The 1955 City Directory listed the following businesses and locations: Fewel Buick, 3317 Fifth Street; Smith's Bakery, Inc., 2730 Sixth Street; Strayhorn Funeral Home, 406 Twenty-fifth Avenue; Wise & Smylie, Inc., 317–20 Rosenbaum Building; Burns & Burns (Beaury C. and Henry Burns) Pan-Am, Eleventh Avenue at A Street; Citizens National Bank, W. Shirley Hiatt, president; Coker's Gulf Service Station, 2500 Eighth Street; Nunnery Hardware, 2101 Sixth Street; City Garage, Inc., 2103 B Street; Firestone Stores, 2603–07 Seventh Street; Lamb's Garage, 211 Nineteenth Avenue and 1813 Eleventh Street; Mitts Motor Co.; DeSoto Plymouth, 809 Twenty-first Avenue; Reliable Chevrolet Co., 2701 Sixth Street; Swartzfager Ford, 420 Twentieth Avenue; Cross Motor Co., Inc., 2700 Sixth Street; Herron Pontiac, 614 Twenty-second Avenue; Hobbs Auto and Supply Co., Inc., 3603 Sixth Street; Mac's Truck Service, 1700 Fourth Street; Merchants & Farmers, 517 Twenty-third Avenue; Mississippi Paint & Glass, 2516 Second Street; the St. Louis Hide Co., Inc., Highway 11 South; Hotel E.F. Young, 500 Twenty-fifth Avenue; Motel Tourist Courts, 4800 Ninth Street; Acme Building & Supply, South Eighth Avenue and Corner of A Street; Mosby's Superior Milk, Cedar Grove Farms, Highway 19; Central Fabricators, 2000 A Street; and WTOK, CBS, NBC, ABC, DuMont Networks, Second Floor, Southern Building.

A.H. Niolon & Son, Inc., Coffee, Teas and Spices, established in 1883. Across the street you can see the Saenger Theater (Temple Theater). *Courtesy of Lauderdale County Department of Archives and History.*

An advertisement in the directory read:

The New Meridian Fair and Cattle Show at Buckwalter Stadium, Now...The official Annual Fair in Meridian, Mississippi...Endorsed by Chamber of Commerce, Agriculture Committee, Meridian Retail Merchants' Association, Superintendent of City Schools, Meridian City Council, Home Demonstration Council, Council of Garden Clubs. 1952 dates—Sept. 29–Oct. 4 (tentative). This is the NEW BIG EVENT in Mississippi...For Details Contact Charles F. Buckwalter or C.B. Rawlings. NEW MERIDIAN FAIR AND CATTLE SHOW, Meridian, Mississippi, P.O. Box 1887, Phone 3-3370

The Mississippi section of the directory included the following:

> *Mississippi Fair and Dairy Show, Meridian. TOTAL ATTENDANCE: Paid. 50,000; free 15,000. Operated 6 days 6 nights. WEATHER: Good 6 days, 6 nights, RECEIPTS: Gate (less tax) $12,000. CARNIVAL: Gem City Shows; ATTRACTIONS: Acts I front of grandstand. Boyle Woolfolk Agency, 2 days horse racing, 3 days auto races. AID. County aid, $500; ADMINISTRATION: President W. R. Cannady; superintendent of concessions, B. Smuckler. 1952 DATES: 1st week, October tentative.*

> *New Meridian Fair and Cattle Show, Meridian. TOTAL ATTENDANCE, 70,000 estimated. Operated 6 days, 6 nights. WEATHER: Good 6 days, 6*

nights. CARNIVAL: Gooding Great. ATTRACTIONS: Ernie Young Night Revue in front of grandstand. 1952 dates; 2nd week in September, tentative

Meridian, Mississippi Fair and Dairy Show. GRANDSTAND CAPACITY; 3,000. Size of race track, half-mile. Plant is rented for: Big car races, hot rod races, midget auto races, harness races, stock car races, thrill shows, rodeos, motorcycle races, circus show lot. COLISEUM (INDOOR ARENA): Available for rental for: Rodeos, ice shows, circuses, stageshows, trade shows.

The Country Music Festival, according to the *Country Music Spectacular Jimmie Rodgers Memorial* brochure, was held annually on the third Monday through Thursday in June. The committees for the 1959 festival included well-known local personalities Lon Smith, Virginia Shine, Carl Fitzgerald, Eddie Holliday, Don Partridge, Mary Alpha Johnson, Gillespie V. "Sonny" Montgomery, T.E. "Shorty" McWilliams, James Skelton, Billy McWilliams, Lloyd Royal, Ernest Pigford and Earl Aycock. Included on the program committee were such personalities as Ernest Tubb and Hank Snow. Some of the sponsoring clubs were the Meridian Restaurant Association, American Legion, Lauderdale County Teachers Association, Meridian

Mary Aycock, G.V. "Sonny" Montgomery and Earl Aycock at the Junior Auxiliary Ball when Sonny was crowned king. *Courtesy of Mary Aycock.*

Moose Lodge, General Council of Garden Clubs and Meridian City Council. Distinguished guests would be Ted Mack, Mrs. Jimmie Rodgers, Governor J.P. Coleman, Frank Clements (former governor of Tennessee), Mrs. Anita Rodgers Court and Jimmie Dale Court. On Monday, June 15, three separate County Music Talent contests began at 7:30 p.m. with the giant street square dance on Fifth Street between Twenty-first and Twenty-second Avenues beginning at 9:00 p.m. The talent show carried into the second day of the festival. Wednesday was the night of "Banquet for the Stars" at the Lamar Hotel and the Talent Elimination Contest. Thursday was the Jimmie Rodgers Day Parade, complete with a memorial service at the Jimmy Rodgers Monument, a Keesler Field Band concert and a by-invitation-only fish fry. The Country Music Spectacular Show continued with the "Top Talent" winner and music celebrities Hank Snow, Marty Robbins, Ferlin Husky, Ernest Tubb, Johnny Cash, Ray Price, Jimmie Davis, Justin Tubb, Charlie Walker, Mac Wiseman, Hank Locklin, the Browns and more. Businesses helping to sponsor the event were Brookshire's Ice Cream, Meridian Hotel, Rose Jewelry Co., Pet Daily Products Company, Moore's Music Center, Reliable Chevrolet, Hardin's Better Bakers, Swartzfager Ford Co., the Borden Company, Lamar Hotel, Dement Printing Co., Central

Jimmie Rodgers Parade in the mid-1950s. *Courtesy of Lauderdale County Department of Archives and History.*

Fabricators, Smith Bakery, Mississippi Beverage Co., Magnolia Beer Distributors, Mitchell Distributing Co., Gower Printing, Southern Pipe and Supply Co. and Lauderdale County Wholesale Petroleum Association, which included a few familiar names like L.L. Majure, Burns & Burns, Cliff Walker, L.B. Paine, L.J. Fruge and Neil Rosenbaum.

The event was cosponsored by the Country Music Association (CMA), which formed in 1958. The brochure of this Nashville association stated, "Through the efforts of Meridian's own Dudley V. (Vic) Skinner, general chairman of the Sixth Annual Jimmie Rodgers Day—County Music Festival, the CMA decided to combine its own next big show with the big event here and make the Meridian Attraction the 'biggest and best of its kind' in the world."

Jimmie Rodgers was honored by a thirteen-cent Jimmie Rodgers (1897–1933) stamp, which became available in Meridian on May 24, 1978.

Also, during the 1950s, theater entrepreneur Lloyd Royal produced two full-length motion picture films, making him the first producer to make full-length films in Mississippi. *Jesse James' Women* (1954) starred Don "Red" Barry and Peggie Castle. *Frontier Woman* (1956) starred Royal's wife, Ann Kelly, Cindy Carson and Lance Fuller. Award-winning actor and producer Ron Howard was the baby in *Frontier Woman*, making this his first film. According to Monte Royal, son of Lloyd Royal, *Frontier Woman* was filmed at Dunn's Falls in Lauderdale County. *Natchez Trace* was made in 1960, starring Zachary Taylor, William Campbell, Irene James and Royal's wife, Ann Kelly. Another of Royal's productions was a comedy of errors filmed in Meridian and included young sons Monte and Kelly, as well as Elliott Street, who later became an actor in television shows such as *Mayberry R.F.D.*, *Love American Style*, *Cade's County*, *Ironside*, *The Mod Squad*, *Hawaii Five-0*, *Kung Fu*, *Serpico* and *The Rockford Files* and movies like *The Legend of Bagger Vance* and *Runaway Jury*.

Frontier Woman, produced by Lloyd Royal. *Courtesy of Monte and Connie Royal.*

FREEDOM SUMMER

The '60s

With a population of 49,374, per the 1960 census, Meridian was the first city in the state to win all ten Merit Awards in the Mississippi Economic Council's statewide Merit Community Development Program. Meridian was also the first city in the state to adopt a council–city manager plan of government.

The Vietnam War, the Hippie Generation, the Cuban Missile Crisis and the women's and civil rights movements made the 1960s some of the nation's most turbulent years. They would also be the most challenging years for Lauderdale County and the state and remain the most difficult to explain.

Thomas Young grew up in a separate but unequal community knowing that things weren't all together right. But he'd always been told not to question certain things. "You were not supposed to discuss racial differences," he said. He was about fourteen when Emmett Till was killed, and that raised many questions for him. Though grownups would sometimes talk about how black students didn't have new books like the white students, his mother told him, "Brother, just master what's in the book you've got."

"It was always instilled in your mind that you didn't ever want to cross any white people," said Robert J. Ray. He shared how, in department stores, white people were waited on first, and blacks couldn't go into a white restaurant and eat. Instead, they went to the back of the restaurant, ordered, paid for the food and went somewhere else to eat it. "I always noticed that and it angered me," added Ray.

Thomas Young. *Courtesy of Parents for Public Schools.*

A Lauderdale County resident since 1932, Jesse Palmer remembers when his twins were born at Riley Hospital. "They wouldn't keep them in the nursery," he said. Instead, they slept in a basinet beside his wife's bed located in the basement of the hospital.

Dr. Hobert Kornegay, whose private dental practice started in 1948, stated in an oral history conducted by the University of Southern Mississippi: "Teachers couldn't belong to the NAACP during that time. They'd give the money, but they'd use some other name [because] you'd lose your job."

Part of the civil rights movement included Freedom Riders, which consisted of busloads of black and white workers traveling across the South in 1961 to urge the enforcement of federal laws prohibiting discrimination in interstate bus travel. By 1963, four civil rights organizations had been formed: the Student Non-Violent Coordinating Committee (SNCC), the Congress of Racial Equality (CORE), the National Association for the Advancement of Colored People (NAACP) and the Southern Christian Leadership Conference (SCLC). These made up the Congress of Federated

Mayor Cheri Barry at the Forty-seventh Annual Mississippi Civil Rights Martyrs Memorial. *Author's collection.*

Organizations (COFO). COFO would focus on black voter registration in Mississippi, which was below 7 percent, the nation's lowest percentage of black voters while the state had the largest black population. Also to be formed were freedom schools, community centers and the White Community Project headed by approximately thirty southern white students.

Roscoe Jones had watched the integration of Little Rock Central High School in Arkansas on television and had also watched the sit-ins of the Freedom Riders. He saw buses being burned and what was happening in Birmingham with the fire hoses. To his grandmother, with whom he lived, he said, "Mama, I need to get involved. This thing is serious."

Jones said that when he and his grandmother traveled, they had to go to the black bathroom and black waiting rooms and stay in that area, even at the train station. On the train was a black section, and if it was crowded, you stood up. On the bus transit system, it was the same thing. Jones became involved with the civil rights movement when he was thirteen years old, joining the NAACP Youth Council led by Ralph Darden, a black photographer in Meridian.

"Meridian was a very segregated place in the '60s, and we wanted to see a change," said George Smith, who was very active in the movement with his wife, Louise.

But Mississippi, among other southern states, wasn't ready. A June 5, 1964 *Meridian Star* article entitled "Senate Bill Is Aimed at 'Racial Schools'" reported:

> *Jackson, Miss. (UPI)—The Mississippi House was expected to take up a bill this afternoon that could seriously hamper plans by civil right groups to open "freedom schools" around the state this summer.*
>
> *The measure would require anyone holding public meetings or setting up schools or clinics to obtain a license from the state or county board of education.*
>
> *The bill, which passed the Senate yesterday, apparently was aimed at the announced plans of civil rights groups to conduct "freedom schools" over the state to instruct Negroes on voter registration. College students from across the nation were expected to come to Mississippi to take part in the program. The bill, released immediately to the House, would apply to anyone calling a meeting or setting up a class or school "for the purpose of advising, teaching, instruction or informing any person or group." To get a license, an applicant would be required to make an affidavit with the chancery clerk giving his name, address, his employer organization and full information as to the class or type of such schools.*
>
> *"This is the bill that will keep those outsiders from opening up all those voter schools this summer," said Sen. E.K. Collins of Laurel. Senate passage was unanimous.*

In the same newspaper, another headline read, "University Instructed to Hold Up on Entrance Certificate for Negro: "Jackson, Miss. (UPI)—The University of Mississippi was instructed today to defer issuance of any entrance certificate to Negro Cleveland Donald, Jr."

"We had been hearing that CORE was coming to town," said Robert Ray, "and we were warned not to get mixed up with them."

Before receiving the right to vote, said Jesse Palmer, African Americans were required to interpret a section of the U.S. Constitution. Voter registration work in Meridian began in the summer of 1963 by COFO staff people. New Yorkers Michael Schwerner, a member of CORE, and his wife,

Rita, arrived in Meridian in January 1964 to open a COFO office at Fielder & Brooks Drugstore at 2505½ Fifth Street in Meridian, which would serve as headquarters for the Freedom Summer operation. Also opened was a COFO-sponsored community center, where black children socialized and played games and had access to a lending library.

Project director of the CORE Meridian, Mississippi operation from 1964 to 1967, George Smith attended one of the first meetings at First Union Baptist Church. He remembered Mickey Schwerner saying, "Look at me. Even though I'm white, I'm not free. No one man is free until all men are free." Born in the basement at Anderson's Hospital, Smith would later work as an orderly at Anderson's and be recognized as Employee of the Month. The day he received the plaque, Smith and others were arrested for picketing Kress and Newberry Stores. The next day, his supervisor at Anderson's fired him.

Sometime after the Schwerners arrived, Meridian volunteer James Chaney joined as a local volunteer. In April, the Schwerners wrote a letter to the national CORE asking that Chaney become a paid staff member: "We consider him to be part of the Meridian staff…James has never asked us to buy him a cup of coffee, though he has no means of support." COFO workers Mark and Betty Levy from Queens College, New York, also came to Meridian as COFO workers. Also, greatly involved was Joe Morse, from Minnesota, who worked with the movement in Meridian from 1964 to 1968.

From January to May, according to Roscoe Jones, participants learned a lot of techniques on nonviolence and how to do sit-ins. On May 30, 1964,

Roscoe Jones, Freedom School volunteer and youth leader, Meridian. *Courtesy of Mark Levy, Queens College, New York.*

they had their first sit-in at Woolworth in Meridian. There were thirteen of them arrested and taken to city hall, where they were booked and sent to jail. On Sunday, May 31, Fannie Lou Hamer was in the city to speak about the Freedom Democratic Party. Because Roscoe and the others were in jail, at the request of Mickey Schwerner, Fannie Lou came onto the jail premises, where she cried and sang to them outside the barred windows.

"The movement was never about integration," said Jones. "Integration was a byproduct and something that could be controlled. Blacks wanted equality. If we were equal, there didn't have to be integration."

COFO in Meridian operated one of the many Freedom Schools in Mississippi in which forty-five out-of-state volunteers participated and which over thirty-five hundred students attended. Meridian's Freedom School was in the Negro Baptist Seminary, a three-story building that provided sufficient classroom space for one hundred students and provided sleeping spaces for up to twenty staff members. It served as base for the six adjoining counties. The ballpark was utilized for recreational purposes, while the building provided blackboards, telephone, a movie projector and screen and a library of over ten thousand publications. Lessons on citizenship, black history, constitutional rights, political processes and basic academics were taught. Because of the Ku Klux Klan and white resistance, many dangers threatened participation in COFO and its efforts. Each family made the final decision of whether their children attended Freedom Schools. Locals brave enough to lodge COFO workers, cash their checks or rent them space risked their jobs, reputations and lives.

In Obie Clark's transcript with the University of Southern, Mississippi, he remembers Polly Heidelberg's experience with the Klan when she and other COFO members were picketing Winn Dixie:

> *These Klansmen, Wayne Roberts, Lee Roberts and them, came down and set up a counter picket line. So Miss Polly and her group were going clockwise, and they were going counterclockwise. They had their hoods on, in broad open daytime. And Raymond pulled his hood off and stood up to Miss Polly and told her all the things that he would do to her. Miss Polly said it scared her so, she lost control of her body functions and wet her pants.*

New Yorker Andrew Goodman arrived in Meridian on June 20, 1964, after completing a training session in Oxford, Ohio. Schwerner had also attended the training and upon their arrival in Meridian, they learned that the Klan had burned the Mt. Zion Methodist Church, a Freedom School location in Neshoba County. Some of the members had also been beaten. On June 21, Schwerner, Goodman and James Chaney headed to Neshoba County to meet with the church leaders. During this trip, Neshoba County deputy sheriff Cecil Price pulled them over, accused them of speeding and took them to jail. After the three were released, on the ride back home, the Neshoba County law pulled them over again. This time, the Klan was involved, several members being from Meridian, and there would be no release.

Schwerner, Chaney and Goodman never made it back to Meridian.

James Chaney's cousin, Thomas Young, had seen James two or three weeks before Young left for Chicago in 1964. "When I heard about the deaths of Chaney, Schwerner and Goodman, I wondered, had I not left for Chicago, where would I be now?"

COFO worker Jane Adams recorded in her journal on July 8, 1964:

> *Everyone here is armed, but it is a tension of caution, not of fear. One cuts the lights when a car goes by, looks out cautiously and everyone else keeps dancing. We don't travel at all after dark if it can be avoided. But the whites know the FBI is all over; Navy teams are scouring the Area* [for the bodies of Schwerner, Chaney and Goodman].

COFO worker Patti Miller remembered that the bodies of Chaney, Schwerner and Goodman were found on August 4, 1964, because it was the day folk musician Pete Seeger performed to a packed house at Mt. Olive Church in Meridian. It was Seeger who announced the discovery of the bodies that night. Everyone held hands and sang songs of peace.

Andy Goodman was only twenty years old and Michael Schwerner was twenty-four when they were murdered on Rock Cut Road on June 21, 1964. Autopsy records, as evidenced by the *Clarion Ledger* of June 4, 2000, reveal that twenty-one-year-old James Chaney had been viciously tortured and shot several times. All three were buried in an earthen dam on Olen Burrage's property in Neshoba County.

Most only remember James Chaney through the Meridian/Philadelphia freedom fighter tragedy, but Chaney's presence extended elsewhere in Mississippi, as noted by Freedom worker Winson Hudson:

> *James Chaney stayed with us on and off and Michael Schwerner stayed with Dovie a while, before they was killed in June. Chaney and Theodis stayed in jail in Canton for a while and laughed about a big dog that was near them and would growl when they would move. Theodis stayed thirty-two days and Chaney might have got out a little bit ahead of him. Now, this was before they went to Oxford, Ohio, for the training... Then things got worse when the workers—Chaney, Schwerner, and Goodman—were murdered.*

Years later, James Chaney's little brother, Ben, would have this to say in *Freedom's Children: Young Civil Rights Activists Tell Their Own Stores* by Ellen Levine:

> *We lived across the street from a white family. From my side of the street on, it was the black community, and from their side of the street, it was the white community. Up until the time I was about ten years old, I always played with those white kids. But once I became ten, their parents came straight out and told me they didn't want me playing with their kids no more.*

Councilman Jesse Palmer said, "James Chaney was the most courteous young man that you could find anywhere. He was one you would've loved to have as a son. He was well-spoken and articulate."

Roscoe Jones said that Mickey Schwerner was "committed to nonviolence. One of the things he demanded was that if you could not be nonviolent, don't get into the movement."

But what kind of person was Mickey Schwerner? "He was one of the nicest guys you ever wanted to meet. He never met a stranger [and] was very responsible and not the type of guy to be careless in sending anyone out."

Reverend Duncan M. Gray Jr. had been actively involved in race equality in Cleveland and Oxford, Mississippi, before arriving in Meridian in 1965 to be rector of St. Paul's Episcopal Church. His oral history transcript with USM states that after the passage of the Civil Rights Law in 1964, the Mississippi

Council on Human Relations, on which he served as a board member, held the first integrated dinner at the King Edward Hotel in Jackson.

On December 4, 1964, the FBI arrested twenty-one suspects on federal conspiracy charges in connection with the murders of the three civil rights workers, charging nineteen with conspiring to deprive the three men of their constitutional rights. The following nineteen defendants were indicted on February 28, 1967: Bernard Akin, Jimmy Arledge, E. G. "Hop" Barnett, Horace Doyle Barnette, Travis Maryn Barnette, Klan Imperial Wizard Sam Bowers, Olen Burrage, James Thomas "Pete" Harris, Frank Herndon, James Edward Jordan, Edgar Ray Killen, Billy Wayne Posey, Neshoba County deputy sheriff Cecil Price, Neshoba County sheriff Lawrence Rainey, Alton Wayne Roberts, Jerry McGrew Sharpe, Jimmy Snowden, Herman Tucker and Philadelphia patrolman Richard Willis.

Of these, eighteen defendants went to federal trial in Meridian on October 7. On October 20, the jury convicted the following: Jimmy Arledge, Horace Doyle Barnette, Sam Bowers, Billy Wayne Posey, Cecil Price, Alton Wayne Roberts and Jimmy Snowden. Every conviction would be appealed. Acquitted were Bernard Akin, Travis Maryn Barnette, Olen Burrage, James Thomas "Pete" Harris, Frank Herndon, Lawrence Rainey, Herman Tucker and Richard Willis. Mistrials were declared on E.G. "Hop" Barnette, Edgar Ray Killen and Jerry McGrew Sharpe.

Just out of his teens, Tommy A. Tarrants III met Imperial Wizard Sam Bowers, according to Tarrants's book *He's My Brother: A Black Activist and a Former Klansman Tell Their Stories*, co-authored with John M. Perkins. In 1967, the Klan had launched terrorist attacks against Jews, blacks and white civil rights workers, bombing Temple Beth Israel in Jackson on September 18 and, two months later, the home of Rabbi Perry Nussbaum. Also bombed were the homes of Dr. William T. Bush, dean of Tougaloo College, and Robert Kochtitzky, both of Jackson.

To avoid being arrested on a National Firearms Act violation and other charges, Tarrants fled for North Carolina, coming out only to meet with Klan members. Between January and May, there had been terrorist attacks in Meridian, including the bombing of Temple Beth Israel on May 28, 1968.

On June 30, Tarrants and Kathy Ainsworth planned to bomb the home of Meridian resident Meyer Davidson. However, Alton Wayne Roberts, a defendant in the Chaney, Goodman and Schwerner case, and Raymond

Roberts made a deal with the FBI by providing full details of the coming bombing. When Tarrants and Ainsworth arrived at the Davidson home, authorities lay in wait. Kathy Ainsworth was killed in the crossfire. Tarrants, though severely wounded, survived to serve time in Parchman State Penitentiary. After his release, he became co-pastor of an interracial church in Washington, D.C., and a strong advocate for race reconciliation.

Obie Clark's oral history also shared that in 1969, twelve black churches in Meridian were burned or bombed in a six-month period, and most didn't have insurance. For those that had insurance, the insurance had been canceled. Those that tried to get insurance couldn't.

A group of ministers organized a biracial committee called the Committee of Conscience. One of the committee members was Reverend Duncan Gray. Gray said in his USM history that this biracial committee raised money to rebuild churches that had been bombed or burned and tried to *bring some measure of reconciliation and healing to the community*.

Roscoe Jones entering the old COFO office in Meridian. *Author's collection.*

All appeals by the convicted defendants in the Chaney, Schwerner and Goodman case had failed. On March 19, 1970, the defendants were in federal custody. Bowers and Roberts had received ten-year sentences; Price and Posey, six years; and Arledge, Snowden and Horace Doyle Barnette, three years. However, no one served more than six years.

Not until 2005 was Neshoba County defendant Edgar Ray Killen convicted of manslaughter in the Chaney, Goodman and Schwerner case in Neshoba County Circuit Court.

George Smith and his wife, Louise, who marched with Dr. King and worked with people of the movement, including James Chaney, make an annual pilgrimage from Fort Wayne to Mississippi to speak at the memorial service for Chaney, Goodman and Schwerner in Meridian.

"Democracy says that all are created equal and are endowed by certain inalienable rights: life, liberty and the pursuit of happiness," said Roscoe Jones. "Slavery had been abolished. We weren't dealing with three-fourths of a man anymore. We were dealing with men, women and children."

RISING AGAIN

By 1967, fewer than 3 percent of Mississippi's black children attended classes with white children. Between 1966 and 1970, according to *Mississippi History Now*, the number of private schools in Mississippi increased from 121 to 236, with enrollment into these schools tripling. Evidence shows that the majority of the fleeing population was in black-majority districts, while in white-majority districts fewer whites fled to private schools.

In Meridian, downtown businesses such as Sears Roebuck & Co. and J.C. Penney were relocating to freestanding buildings or into new shopping centers on the outskirts of town, such as Broadmoor and Cloverleaf shopping centers.

Gillespie V. "Sonny" Montgomery had served in the Mississippi House of Representatives from 1956 to 1966 and as a U.S. representative from 1967 to 1997. In 1984, Montgomery revamped the original GI Bill enacted on June 22, 1944, by Franklin D. Roosevelt. Montgomery realized the importance of education to the proficiency of the nation's security and military. The Montgomery GI Bill ensured educational benefits to all who served in the military.

Since 1904, Wesley House has survived many difficult times. In the 1960s, when threatened with closure, Nell Grissom stepped in as a volunteer and ended up serving as director for over forty years. Under her direction, Wesley House thrived. In 1986, daughter Ginger Stevens, who had grown up in Wesley House around her mother's work, became the director. Since then,

Threefoot Building and the Marks, Rothenberg and Company Department Store before renovation. *Courtesy of Lauderdale County Department of Archives and History.*

the mission has expanded into the areas of education, victim and health services and community services, such as scouting, clearing house, clothes closet, parenting, food pantry and much more. Wesley House is also the site for the East Mississippi Sexual Assault Center.

Meridian Naval Air Station (NAS) became a full naval air station in 1968. The Naval Technical Training Center, known as the Stennis Center, is named after U.S. senator John C. Stennis, guest speaker for the July 14, 1961 opening ceremony. Over eight thousand acres occupy the main base of NAS Meridian. An additional four thousand acres make up Williams Field and the target facility SEARAY.

Wade Jones, executive director of the East Mississippi Business Development Corporation (EMBDC), said that Lauderdale County's past and future pertaining to flight is symbolic of what has occurred in the area: the air national guard, Lockheed Martin, Meridian Naval Air Station and Key Field, with its ten-thousand-foot runway and 130-acre site.

Panoramic view of Meridian from the highest point. *Author's collection.*

He also said that because of its proximity to Dallas, Atlanta, Memphis and New Orleans, along with the I-20/59 interchange and the railroad, Lauderdale County is the perfect location for distribution warehousing. This is also evidenced by a report released by Chicago Consulting identifying the top distribution networks in the country. Meridian, Mississippi, was included in that report because it is located within a four-hundred-mile radius of half the nation's population.

In addition, said Jones, Lauderdale County has one of the largest wood baskets, in terms of density, soft woods and hard woods, making it abundant in energy resources that can be converted into biomass, a renewable energy source.

A lot of changes have taken place in the timber marketplace since Jim McInnis took over McInnis Lumber Co., Inc., in the 1980s, such as railroad deregulations, the advent of the wholesale distributor concept and the discontinuation of certain wholesaler discounts. Evolving from retail sales to industrial sales has been crucial to the success of McInnis Lumber. With so much emphasis on green living, the reputation of forest product industry isn't as good as it should be. McInnis states that trees have always been a crop, a renewable resource, and that virtually every piece of a tree can be used—the bark, the sawdust, the shavings, the lumber itself, pine needles, etc. Over-cutting and not replanting are what cause major problems.

Reared on a farm in Lauderdale off the Lauderdale–Kewanee Road, Ralph Morgan had always wanted to be a logger and a cowboy. At the age of six, he drove his first log truck constructed of apple boxes by a few childhood friends. He loaded it with firewood and drove all through his house. Now, Ralph Morgan Logging is a family business consisting of twelve logging trucks and includes his wife, Elizabeth, known to everyone as "Lib," and their son, Johnny Ralph. The Morgans own and manage fifty-four hundred acres of timberland, pastureland and prime real estate. Morgan received the Mississippi Outstanding Logger award in 1990 and was a regional finalist in the Forest Resources Association's national recognition.

The Ralph Morgan Rodeo, affiliated with the Professional Rodeo Cowboys Association (PRCA), is one of the South's most highly acclaimed rodeos. Established over thirty-five years ago, this rodeo is held every April and August in Lauderdale with more than 140 contestants competing in saddle team roping, steer wrestling, bronco riding, bull riding, bareback riding, calf roping and women's barrel racing. Once a rodeo competitor himself, Morgan retired after winning the Tri-State Rodeo Championship in calf roping three times and in steer wrestling twice. In 1982, Ralph Morgan and James Harper formed Harper and Morgan Rodeo Co., which put on twenty-one shows a year in mostly the Southeast. Morgan's award-winning rodeo livestock made it to the National Finals Rodeo and won numerous Southeastern circuit livestock awards.

Many Meridian entrepreneurs began at the bottom and worked themselves to the top like the late Bud Robinson, founder of Robinson Electric Supply, which opened in June 1975. Originally from Whynot, Bud's career began with Sammy Davidson. Because of his mother's illness, Robinson had quit school to help make a living for his family. As a teen, he swept floors in the Southern Electric warehouse, working his way up to managing over fifteen branches of the company. Robinson remained with Southern Electric for over twenty years. With dreams of opening his own business, Robinson sold everything he owned and obtained financing from Quitman banker Jack Pogue. Daughter Debbie (Bridgmon) was the second employee of Robinson Electric and remains active in the business along with her little sister, Melanie Moss. Debbie worked for her daddy at Southern Electric during the summers and after school. When Debbie was graduating from high school, Bud decided to get his diploma, too, through the GED program. He became the first student to pass each part of the exam without taking the required classes. Robinson Electric has nine locations across the nation and has been named one of the nation's top two hundred electrical distributors by the National Association of Electrical Distributors (NAED).

In October 1975, Jimmy and Ann Alexander stepped into an electrical business of their own, thanks to a partnership with Meridian businessman

Henry Burns. As a woman, Ann had to prove herself in a predominantly male world of construction. She now serves as chairman of EMBDC, volunteering her time on other boards, such as the Mississippi Arts & Entertainment Center (MAEC) and Hope Village. A&B Electric has enjoyed thirty-six years of growth and stability.

Southern Pipe & Supply Company, one of the nation's largest privately held, independent wholesalers of plumbing and heating and air-conditioning materials, has remained a family-owned business in Meridian, Mississippi, since the early 1930s. The grandson of Founder Louis Davidson, Marty Davidson, became president at the age of twenty-eight.

Across Mississippi, nearly fifteen thousand people are employed in the metal fabrication/steel industry, with steel companies in Lauderdale County playing a huge part in the numbers. According to Tommy Dulaney, after World War II, Sammy Davidson and Melvin Smith, who was the owner of Meridian Oxygen, formed Central Fabricators on Eighth Street. "That's where fabrication got started in Meridian," he said. About 1950, Jack Bates, from Mobile, went to work for Central Fabricators and later formed Bates Steel. In the mid-1950s, Dewey Tucker bought Central Fabricators, which became Tucker Steel. Magnolia Steel began fabricating rebar in 1962. With the financial backing of Tommy Webb and Sammy Davidson, Tommy Dulaney founded Structural Steel Services in Meridian in the mid-1970s, after working at Bates Steel for almost ten years. Around the same time, E.M. "Hoot" Gipson" founded Gipson Steel after working for twenty-three years in the structural steel industry. Slay Steel and Henderson Steel began in the 1980s.

When Manny Mitchell's grandfather, E.J. Mitchell, emigrated from Lebanon to America, he could only afford to bring his oldest child, leaving

E.J. Mitchell sign.
Author's collection.

seven others in Lebanon. Settling in Meridian in the 1920s, the Mitchells opened a general store in 1931 in the vicinity of the current Mitchell Distributing Company, an Anheuser Busch distributor. They had six more children, including Mann Mitchell, Manny's father, and Bilbo Mitchell, father to Meridian attorney Bilbo Mitchell. Mann and Bilbo Sr. worked for Sammy Davidson, whose many ventures included the beer business. Newton County was wet, and Lauderdale County was dry. Mann traveled to New Orleans to pick up loads of beer to be run on the beer route from Newton County. When Lauderdale County became wet, Mann became a distributor of Falstaff Beer in Lauderdale County and later a distributor of Budweiser. Because Budweiser wanted an exclusive with the company, the company was forced to separate. Bilbo took Falstaff, which at the time was the most popular brand, and Mann took Budweiser. The monument above the old grocery store doorway reading "E.J. Mitchell 1931" now hangs on the Mitchell Distributing Company building, located on the old E.J. Mitchell homeplace. Mitchell Companies include Mitchell Distributing Co., Mitchell Signs, M-Prints, National Scrubwear, Inc., and Southern LED Solutions.

Through the 1940s and much of the '50s, the preferred location of the car dealerships, including Reliable Chevrolet and Swartzfager Ford, had been downtown in the Fifth and Sixth Street areas. In 1957, Reliable relocated to Tom Bailey Drive. About 1970, Nelson Hall purchased the interest in the dealership, renamed it Nelson Hall Chevrolet and is still doing business in the same location.

Hartley Peavey, founder of Peavey Electronics in the spring of 1965, began the company with the $8,000 his father had reserved for Hartley's college education. Hand crafting amps in his father's basement, Peavey expanded his business into the only American company that manufactures every link in the audio chain, including P.A. Systems, guitars, amps, digital electronics, software and accessories. Peavey has been inducted into the Mississippi Musicians Hall of Fame, Mississippi Innovators Hall of Fame, International Music Products Association Hall of Fame, the Rock Walk of Fame and the Vintage Guitar Hall of Fame. A recipient of the Musikmesse International Press Association Hall of Fame Lifetime Achievement award, Peavey has also received an honorary doctor of creative and performing arts degree from Mississippi State University.

Hobert Kornegay became the first African American elected to the Meridian City Council in 1977 and in 1985 became the first black supervisor

Sela Ward Walk of Fame Star. *Author's collection.*

in Lauderdale County. Activist Charles Young had been affiliated with Medgar and Charles Evers, Dr. Aaron Henry and Fannie Lou Hammer. He was the first African American to join Meridian's chamber of commerce. He was elected as a Democrat to the House of Representatives in 1979.

Anderson's and Rush Hospital continue as two major healthcare and employer sectors in Mississippi. Though Riley Memorial Hospital was instrumental in Meridian's medical mecca, it went another way to guarantee Dr. Franklin Gail Riley's vision. In 1998, the hospital was sold, and the proceeds established the Riley Foundation.

The land where the Masonic Widows and Orphans Home was located is now home to Hope Village for Children, founded by award-winning actress and Meridian's own Sela Ward. In 2001, Peavey House, a shelter for abused and neglected children, relocated onto the thirty acres. Hilltop House for Boys and Hilltop House for Girls relocated there in 2002, the opening year of Hope Village. The original funding efforts of Hope Village were made possible through a Riley Foundation grant. The Hope Village Administration is located in the house that was bequeathed to the organization by the late Jack Malone of Meridian. According to Tina Aycock, executive director of Hope Village for Children, this house, built in the 1920s, was the first in Meridian to have central air and heat.

Carousels Abound, a fundraiser for Hope Village, was a public art project originated by Jamie Cater and Debbie Martin. Inspired by animal art found in major cities, such as the Chicago cows and the New Orleans fish, carousel horses

Bonita Lakes Carousel horse "Fantasy Filly," painted by Jessie Brashier. *Author's collection.*

were the perfect choice for Meridian because of the historic Dentzel Carousel in Highland Park. Over seventy-five painted carousel horses have been placed around Lauderdale County, with sponsorship funds going to Hope Village.

The Mississippi Industrial Heritage Museum gained the title to Soulé Steam Works in 2002. The first Soulé Live Steam Festival was held in October 2003 showcasing the history of steam engines. This annual festival has expanded to a two-day event.

Other annual festivals and events include the Martin Luther King celebration held each January and "Juneteenth," which celebrates the day of June 19, 1865, when Union soldiers, led by Major General Gordon Granger, announced the end of the Civil War and the freeing of slaves. The Threefoot Festival, sponsored by the Meridian Council for the Arts, is held the first weekend in April.

In 1961, Jimmie Rodgers became one of the first three artists inducted into the Country Music Hall of Fame. In 1970, he was inducted into the Nashville Songwriters Hall of Fame and into the Rock and Roll Hall of Fame in 1986. He received the first marker on the Mississippi Country Music Trail and has also been honored with a Mississippi Blues Trail marker. For over ten years, Jimmie's sister-in-law, Meridian resident Elsie McWilliams, cowrote many of Jimmie Rodgers's songs. She was inducted

Britt Gully honoring Jimmie Rodgers at the Country Music Trails Marker dedication. *Author's collection.*

into the Nashville Songwriters Hall of Fame in 1979. The Jimmie Rodgers Festival has been held since 1953.

Stories of other successful homegrown businesses like Long's Wholesale, Burns & Burns, Maples Gas, Fruge Oil, Dowdle Gas, Sanders Gas, Meyer & Rosenbaum Insurance and Berry and Gardner Funeral Home saturate Lauderdale County's history, demonstrating the strength, determination and faith of its people.

For years, only the ghosts from Meridian's past would occupy the abandoned downtown structures. Some buildings lost to neglect have been demolished, but others are being resuscitated, such as the Grand Opera House. Thanks to a partnership between Mississippi State University and the Riley Foundation, the Grand Opera House reopened in 2006 as the MSU Riley Center and is again one of the South's premier entertainment venues. The historic J.J. Newberry and S.H. Kress Buildings are another phase of the MSU/Riley partnership and will serve the MBA division of the MSU Meridian Campus.

Becky Farley, executive director of the Riley Foundation, emphasized the arts and education component of the foundation's grant program. "Through our partnership with Mississippi State University," said Becky, "we have granted around $23 million in scholarships and for downtown Meridian."

Dennis Sankovich, executive director of the MSU Riley Center, said that part of what MSU Riley does is train teachers in arts integration, bringing in the arts as an educational tool that reaches the whole human being. "We have surgically removed the arts and literature from the classroom and are teaching to the tests."

Charlotte Tabereaux, MSU Riley Center Education director, said, "If you walk by a classroom and see children dancing and doing music or painting, you think that classroom might be out-of-control. But it's not. Truly, that's the way we all learn."

Formed in 1961, the original Meridian Symphony Orchestra (MSO), under the thirty-year direction of Vernon Raines, made its debut performance on April 1, 1962, and celebrated its fiftieth year in 2011. MSO is one of five professional symphonies in Mississippi and has established a strings program with plans to add woodwind and brass instruction.

Mississippi's largest community theater and the only theater to have a youth division is Meridian Little Theatre. Founded in 1932, its first production was in Highland Park, making it one of the South's oldest subscription-based community theaters.

Today's Front Street looking south. *Author's collection.*

The Sucarnochee Revue, broadcasted nationwide and aired on Mississippi Public Television, performs live at the historical Temple (Saenger) Theater, known now as the Temple Theater for the Performing Arts. A longtime lover of historic theaters, Roger Smith bought the Temple from the Hamasa Shriners in 2009. Breaking down racial stereotypes is one of his goals. "We have to embrace diversity in our differences and not be afraid of it," he said. "We all have something unique to offer."

At the Temple on July 22, 2010, Mississippi secretary of state Delbert Hosemann announced Meridian as the first city to receive the state's entertainment district designation. The district extends from Interstate 20/59 and includes the old Village Fair Mall, the downtown and the midtown areas of Meridian.

MBA students of the MSU Meridian campus conducted an apartment study and survey in potential demand for downtown living in Meridian. They found that downtown apartments maintain an 85 percent occupancy rate. These living quarters included the Front Street apartments, the Rosenbaum Building condominiums and the Union Hotel apartments. Meridian Main Street executive director John McClure expects growth in specialty, entertainment and eating facilities due to the growing downtown residencies and student

Mississippi Arts and Entertainment Center (MAEC) plaque. *Author's collection.*

City Hall under renovation with a fence painted by children during the 2011 Threefoot Festival. *Author's collection.*

population. Another aspect of revitalization is the return of mom and pop shops located on the ground floor with the owners' living quarters above.

Just as Elvis was Tupelo's ticket to tourism, Jimmie Rodgers is Lauderdale County's. Relative to tourism, executive director of Lauderdale County tourism Suzy Johnson said the challenge is not in creating or building tourism but in promoting events in the county that draw tourism.

The future Mississippi Arts and Entertainment Center (MAEC) will be located in downtown Meridian. Honoring the state's biggest asset, the arts and entertainment industry, MAEC will be a perfect example of how past, present and future depend on one another. From Jimmie Rodgers to Jimmy Ruffin, from Alvin Childress to Sela Ward, just the number of famous people whose roots dig into the soil of Lauderdale County is amazing.

Many cultures, religions and ethnic groups continue to build Lauderdale County.

"A community can't thrive if you don't support it," said Ann Alexander. "It's a person's responsibility to get involved. It's a heart thing."

"We have to get away from ethnicity and find what we have in common," said Thomas Young. "The key is to overcome and conquer. If you don't overcome, you will be conquered."

"I love diversity," said Mayor Cheri Barry. "It shows character, charisma, and heritage. When you see people of different cultures and backgrounds working together, you see a community that will grow."

Appendix

NOTABLE LAUDERDALE COUNTY NATIVES

John Luther Adams, composer
Susan Akin, 1986 Miss America
John Alexander, New York Metropolitan Opera star
Howard Bahr, author
Moe Bandy, country music singer
Dennis Ray "Oil Can" Boyd, former Major League Baseball pitcher
James Chaney, 1964 civil rights martyr
Alvin Childress, actor, lead role in *Amos 'n' Andy Show*
Mike Compton, musician
George Cummings, guitarist, songwriter
Paul Davis, singer
Chris Ethridge, bassist, songwriter
Bill Evans, five-time Emmy-award-winning meteorologist for WABC-TV, New York City
Winifred Hamrick Farrar, poet laureate of Mississippi
John C. Fleming, physician, author of *Preventing Addiction*
Steve Forbert, recording artist
Dill Harris, fictional character in Harper Lee's *To Kill A Mockingbird.*
Ty Herndon, country music singer
Al Key, aviator and former mayor of Meridian
Fred Key, aviator
Greg Keyes, author
Diane Ladd, actress
Lisa Raye McCoy, actress
Derrick McKey, professional basketball player

Elsie McWilliams, songwriter
Samuel Mockbee, architect, winner of MacArthur Fellow award
Gillespie V. "Sonny" Montgomery, late U.S. representative
Hartley Peavey, electrical engineer, founder of Peavey Electronics
Jay Powell, Major League Baseball player
Gail Robinson, Metropolitan Opera star
Jimmie Rodgers, country music singer
David Ruffin, former lead singer of The Temptations
Jimmy Ruffin, singer
Pat Sansone, multi-instrumentalist in bands Wilco and the Autumn Defense
Jerry Turner, TV anchorman
Sela Ward, award-winning actress/author
Gayle Dean Wardlow, Delta Blues historian and author
Skeeter Webb, professional baseball player
James Wheaton, actor, director and writer
Hayley N. Williams, lead singer of Paramore
Papa Williams, baseball player
Al Wilson, singer, drummer
E.F. Young Jr., founder of E.F. Young Jr. Manufacturing Company

BIBLIOGRAPHY

Allen, Felicity. *Jefferson Davis, Unconquerable Heart*. Columbia: University of Missouri Press, 1999.

Allison, W.G. *Indian Towns and Trails in Lauderdale County and Adjacent Counties.* State of Mississippi Department of Archives and History, n.d.

Atkinson, William B., ed. *The Physicians and Surgeons of the United States.* Philadelphia: Charles Robson, 1878.

Axelrod, Alan. *The Complete Idiot's Guide to the Civil War*. New York: Alpha, a Division of Penguin Group, 1998.

Bearss, Margie Riddle. *Sherman's Forgotten Campaign, The Meridian Expedition.* Pembina, ND: Gateway Press, 1987.

Bettersworth, John K. *Mississippi.* Austin, TX: Steck Company, 1959.

Boyd, Gregory A. *Family Maps of Lauderdale County, Mississippi.* Arphas Publishing Co. Lauderdale County Department of Archives and History.

Brieger, James F., comp. *Hometown, Mississippi.* Meridian Public Library, n.d.

Burt, Jesse, and Robert E. Ferguson. *Indians of the Southeast: Then and Now.* Nashville, TN: Abingdon Press, 1973.

Busbee, Westley F., Jr. *Mississippi: A History*. Wheeling, IN: Harlan Davidson Publisher, 2005.

Cabaniss, Allen. *Grand Lodge of Mississippi, Free and Accepted Masons*, October 17, 1982.

Civil War Chronicle

Claiborne, John Francis Hamtramck. *The Life and Times of Gen. Sam Dale.* Charlston, SC: BiblioLife, 2009.

Clarke, Hewitt. *Thunder at Meridian.* Spring, TX: Lone Star Press, 1995.

Condensed History of the Great Yellow Fever Epidemic of 1878. Memphis, TN: S.C. Toof & Co., Printers and Lithographers, 1879.

Cushman, Horatio Bardwell. *History of the Choctaw, Chickasaw and Natchez, Indians*. Greenville, TX: Headlight Printing House, 1899.

Davis, Kenneth C. *Don't Know Much About the Civil War.* New York: William Morrow and Company, Inc., 1996.

Davis, Ronald L.F., PhD. "Creating Jim Crow: In-Depth Essay." http://www.jimcrowhistory.org/history/creating2.htm. Dawson, James T. *John C. Dunn & Dunn's Falls.* Lauderdale County Department of Archives and History, n.d.

———. *Local Histories: Whynot*. Lauderdale County Department of Archives and History, n.d.

Dawson, Jim. *Bits and Pieces.* Vol. 1. Meridian, MS: Lauderdale County Department of Archives and History, Inc., 1995.

———. *History of Lauderdale County, Mississippi School System.* Edited by Doug Little and Birdie Mae Rogers. Lauderdale County Department of Archives and History, 1988.

Decade of Triumph-The 40s. New York: Time-Life Books, 1999.

DeRosier, Arthur H., Jr. *The Removal of Choctaw Indians.* New York: Harper Torchbook, 1972.

Downing, Alexander G. *Downing's Civil War Diary.* Charleston, SC: printed by C. Stephen Badgley, Createspace, 2010.

DuBose, John Campbell. *Sketches of Alabama History*. Philadelphia: Eldredge & Brother, 1901.

Dunbar, Rowland, and A.G. Sanders, eds. *Mississippi Provincial Archives 1729–1740 French Dominion*. Jackson: Mississippi Department Archives and History Press, n.d.

East Mississippi State Hospital Centennial Program. Sponsored by the Mississippi Department of Mental Health and Mental Health Association in Lauderdale County.

Edmiston, Fred W. "1854–1856: A Directory of Marion." Ms. compiled by from the *Lauderdale Republican*.

———. *Lauderdale, Mississippi's Empire County.* Vol. 1, *The Early Years, 1830–1865.* Meridian, MS: Lauderdale County Department of Archives and History, Inc., 2005.

———. *Meridian at War.* Lauderdale County Department of Archives and History, n.d.

Encyclopedia of Mississippi Indians, Tribes, Nations, Treaties of the Southeastern Woodlands Area. Somerset Publishers, Inc., 2000.

Fairley, Laura Nan, and James T. Dawson. *Paths to the Past Meridian: Lauderdale County.* Department of Archives and History, Inc., 1988.

———. *Paths to the Past: An Overview History of Lauderdale County.* Jackson, MS: Quail Ridge Press, 1988.

Fickle, James E. *Mississippi Forests and Forestry.* University Press of Mississippi, 2001.

Fike, Claude E. "William H. Hardy: An Extraordinary Life." In *The Hattiesburg Story: 100 Years of Growth.* Hattiesburg, MS: Hattiesburg American, 1982.

Halbert, H.S. "Story of the Treaty of Dancing Rabbit." *Publications of the Mississippi Historical Society* 6 (1902): 373–402.

Hardy, Toney. *No Compromise with Principle.* New York: American Book-Stratford Press, Inc., 1946.

Hardy, W.H. "Recollections of Reconstruction in East and Southeast Mississippi." *Publications of the Mississippi Historical Society* 4 (1902): 105–32.

Haynes, Robert V. *The Mississippi Territory and the Southwest Frontier, 1795–1817.* Lexington: University Press of Kentucky, 2010.

History of Citizens National Bank, Meridian, Miss., 1888–1987. Lauderdale County Department of Archives and History.

History of Meridian Fire Department. Lauderdale County Department of Archives and History.

History of Tennessee, Illustrated: Giles, Lincoln, Franklin and Moore Counties. Nashville, TN: Goodspeed Publishing Company, 1979.

Hudson, Winson, and Constance Curry. *Mississippi Harmony: Memoirs of a Freedom Fighter.* New York, NY: Palgrave Macmillan, 2002.

Illustrated Handbook of Meridian, Mississippi. Issued under the auspices of the Meridian Board of Trade and Cotton Exchange, 1907.

In Our 2nd Century, 1870–1970, 100th Year Celebration. Booklet by the Weidmann family at their 100th year celebration.

Jacobs, James B., and Kimberly Potter. *Hate Crimes: Criminal Law and Identity Politics.* Oxford University Press, Inc., 1998.

Johnston, Erle. *Mississippi's Defiant Years, 1953–1973, An Interpretive Documentary with Personal Experiences.* Forest, MS: Lake Harbor Publishers, 1990.

Jones, R.W. "Confederate Cemeteries and Monuments in Mississippi." *Publications of the Mississippi Historical Society* 7 (1904): 87–119.

Jordon, Thomas, and John P. Pryon. *The Campaigns of Lieutenant General N.B. Forrest, and of Forrest's Cavalry.* New York: Blelock and Company, 1868.

Journal of the American Academy for the Preservation of Old-Time Country Music 36 (December 1996).

Journal of the Mississippi Secession Convention, January 1861, Reproduced in Commemoration of the Centennial of the Civil War by the Mississippi Commission on the War between the State 1962. Jackson, MS: E. Barksdale, state printer, 1861.

Keetley, Dawn, and John Pettegrew. *Public Women, Public Words: A Documentary History of American Feminism.* New York: Rowman and Littlefield Publishers, Inc., 2002.

Kennedy, Stetson. *The Klan Unmasked.* Arco Publishers. Reprint, Florida Atlantic University Press, 1990.

Lauderdale Republican

Lawrence, Betty. *A History of Lauderdale Springs, Mississippi.* Meridian, MS: Lauderdale County Department of Archives and History, n.d.

Levine, Ellen. *Freedom's Children; Young Civil Rights Activists Tell Their Own Stores.* New York: Puffin, a division of Penguin Group, 2000.

Lewis, Lloyd B., Dr. *The Impact of the Railroad on Meridian and Lauderdale County, Mississippi.* Sponsored by the Mississippi Humanities Council Scholar in Residence Program and the Lauderdale County Department of Archives and History, n.d.

Marrs, Aaron W. *Railroads in the Old South.* Baltimore, MD: John Hopkins University Press, 2009.

McLemore, Dr. R.A., president of Mississippi College. Interview, April 1961.

McLemore, Richard. *A History of Mississippi.* Vol. I. Jackson: University and College Press of Mississippi, 1973.

"The Memoir of Ben Arthur Davis, 'Those Rugged Years.'" Lauderdale County Department of Archives and History.

Meridian Star

Mississippi State Sovereignty Commission

Mitchell, Dennis J. *A Rich Past, A Vibrant Future, The History & Renovation of the Marks Rothenberg and Grand Opera House Buildings.* Mississippi State University Riley Center for Education and Performing Arts, 2006.

Moody, Anne. *Coming of Age in Mississippi.* New York, NY: Laurel Book, Dell Publishing, n.d.

Music and Sound's Greatest Hits Since 1965. Peavey Electronics Corporation. Lauderdale County Department of Archives and History.

The New Book of Knowledge. Danbury, CT: Grolier Incorporated, 2001.

1908–09 City Directory. Vol. VIII, *Maloney's 1908–1909 Meridian, Miss.* Interstate Publishing Co., 1909.

Our American Century: Prelude to a Century, 1870-1900. Time Life Books, n.d.

Overall Economic Development Program for East Central Mississippi. Newton, MS: East Central Economic Development District, Inc., 1969.

Perkins, John M. *He's My Brother, A Black Activist and a Former Klansman Tell Their Stories.* Grand Rapids, MI: Chosen Books, 1994,

Plantation Diary of H. Blackwood, Overseer of B.F. Moore Plantation; January–July 1859. Lauderdale County Department of Archives and History.

Redlands Fortnightly Club. "Other Fortnightly Clubs in U.S." www.redlandsfortnightly.org.

Riddel, J.A., and J.T. Calhoun. *Lauderdale County Education.* Original printing 1922. Subsequent replica printings: 1977, 1978, 1983 and 1994.

Riley, Franklin L. "Choctaw Land Claims." *Publications of the Mississippi Historical Society* 8 (1904): 302.

Rubin, Richard. *American History of the 20th Century.* Garden City, NY: Byron Preiss Book, Doubleday Direct, Inc., n.d.

Tankersley, Mike. Article. *Southern Loggin' Times*, November 1989.

"The Timber Industry in the Great Depression." Oral history project of the LCDAH and MCC.

Turitz, Leo E., and Evelyn Turitz. *Jews in Early Mississippi.* Jackson: University Press of Mississippi, 1983.

Smith, Allene De Shazo. *Greenwood Leflore and the Choctaw Indians of the Mississippi Valley.* Memphis, TN: C.A. Davis Printing Company, 1951.

Steeples, Douglas W., and David O. Whitten. *Democracy in Desperation: The Depression of 1893.* San Francisco, CA: Greenwood Press, 1998.

Stewart, Robert. *The Illustrated Almanac of Historical Facts.* Upper Saddle River, NJ: Prentice Hall, 1992.

Sydnor, Charles S., and Claude Bennett. *Mississippi History.* New York: Johnson Publishing Company, 1939.

Timme, S. Lee. *Wildflowers of Mississippi.* University Press of Mississippi, 1989.

United States Census Bureau. 1850, 1860, 1870, 1880, 1900 and 1910 U.S. Federal Censuses.

Wall, Barbara Mann, and Arlene Keeling. *Nurses on the Frontline: When 'Disaster Strikes 1878-2010.* New York: Springer Publishing, 2010.

Wilkie, Curtis. *Dixie, A Personal Odyssey Through Events That Shaped the Modern South.* New York: Simon Schuster, Inc., 2001.

Wiltshire, Betty C., comp. *Register of Choctaw Emigrants to the West 1831 and 1832.* Carrollton, MS: Pioneer Publishing Co., 1993.

Work Progress Administration (WPA). Field worker Henry J. Woods, Document #230, "Ear'y Settlement Lauderdale County."

Wright, Richard. *Black Boy.* New York: Harper and Brothers, 1945.

Young, James B., and James M. Ewing. *The Mississippi Public Junior College Story: The First Fifty Years, 1922–1972.* Jackson: University Press of Mississippi, 1978.

ABOUT THE AUTHOR

A lover of history, Richelle Putnam has been an artist-in-residence at schools and at the Girl Scouts of America and has facilitated journaling sessions in prison settings with incarcerated women, worked in libraries, schools, Headstart Programs and Boys and Girls Clubs. A graduate from Gotham's Fiction Certificate Program, she has won writing awards and has been published in many print and online publications. She is a Mississippi Arts Commission (MAC) literary artist and teaching artist and a Mississippi Humanities Council speaker on the therapeutic art of journaling. She has also graduated from three Institute of Children's Literature courses; the Advanced Writing Program of Open College for the Arts in London, England; Writer's Digest Novel Writing Course; England's Poetry Kit Advanced Poetry Course; Gotham Writer's Advanced Poetry Course; and Gotham Writer's Playwriting Course. Her website is www.richelleputnam.net.